PEACE

Discovering Life's Harmony through Relationships

by

Suna Senman

AuthorHouse™ LLC
1663 Liberty Drive
Bloomington, IN 47403
www.authorhouse.com
Phone: 1-800-839-8640

Published by AuthorHouse   07/12/2013

ISBN: 978-1-4772-1261-5 (e)
ISBN: 978-1-4772-1263-9 (hc)
ISBN: 978-1-4772-1262-2 (sc)

Library of Congress Control Number: 2012909657

Front cover photograph by Dr Edward Schork, PhD titled "Turtle in St John, VI"
illustration for chapter "Happiness" is by Sarah Ford titled "Balance"
water color painting and all other drawings are by Suna Senman

This book is printed on acid-free paper.

Contents

Preface ~ ~ ~ vii
The Beginning ~ ~ ~ 1
Peace ~ ~ ~ 9
Honesty ~ ~ ~ 17
Relationships ~ ~ ~ 23
Dream ~ ~ ~ 63
Beauty ~ ~ ~ 79
Truth ~ ~ ~ 87
Love ~ ~ ~ 107
Value ~ ~ ~ 117
Compassion ~ ~ ~ 129
Justice ~ ~ ~ 139
Responsibility ~ ~ ~ 151
Happiness ~ ~ ~ 159
New Being (New Peace Being) ~ ~ ~ 167
About the Author (Back to the Beginning) ~ ~ ~ 173

Preface

Two years after completing my first book, *Being*, I realized that my new book, *Peace*, would be about partnerships. While *Being* is about recognizing and celebrating the fullness of your being as an individual, *Peace* is about creating harmony in life through building healthy relationships.

Relationships constitute the dynamic through which we produce our being, objects and situations. Healthy relationships create healthy things. Relationships that are focused on bringing harmony amidst diversity create peace. Peace is a synchronicity among individuals. Unique individuals that partner to create a greater good are what I call "partnering relationships." Because this book is about creating peace through partnering relationships, you and I will write this book together. I will present my perspective that hopefully stimulates a new insight or reflection from you; and you will write your reflections with each new perspective. Write with hope. Hope is different than fantasy. Hope is a dream that you can see along with the steps to get there and the willingness to take those steps. Fantasy is a dream that you wish to happen to you without you own work. Your hopes will be fulfilled.

We do not know what the results will be, because we are initiating something that will evolve similar to how life's relationships form. The content of this book may be very helpful in giving insight to your other relationships in life. When you have contributed your part sincerely to this text, it will be one of your most important works. You can refer back to your manuscript in times of change, confusion, or simple reflection. This textbook of peace, co-created by you, will reveal the constant truth of who you are, which remains consistent throughout all the many changes of your life.

Everything in life is in a state of change. Life is a process of growth. Some of us are more aware of this course than others. Yet, whether we are aware, the process of change exists and develops us into more of who we are each day.

Take a moment to observe who you are, what others say about you and what you say about yourself in your inner chatter. Paying attention is what is referred to as being mindful. When you are observant and mindful, you get a picture of what is: who you are now and what you are creating. Be honest in recognizing that the world you have around you now is your manifestation through the choices you have made in relationships and actions.

Following are some observation-based questions to consider when looking at the relationships in your life:

- Do I feel supported in life with healthy relationships?
- Which relationships do I feel good about?
- Which relationships seem burdensome?
- If a relationship with one person seems both joyful and burdensome, which dynamics bring joy and which breed disharmony?
- If you had a good relationship that went sour, what happened?
- Is there a relationship with which I feel frustrated?
- Do I feel alone?

Answering the above questions may unearth more questions. Perhaps the concern of life's purpose may come up. You may experience more confusion than clarity at the initial stages of inquiry. Confusion breeds anxiety and my purpose is certainly not to create worry. In the chapters that follow we will stir up the deeper issues, process them, and build clarity together.

Through my work counseling young people and adults, I see a lot of difficulty arise from misunderstandings of what mature independence is. True mature independence is inter-dependence. The statement, "No man is an island," has many layers of meaning that unfold over a lifetime. The mistake that many people make, which often results in stress, anxiety, and depression, is that they adapt a false conviction of believing that they must accomplish everything on their own. The truth is that we are always in relationship with something in anything we do or produce. We will explore this misunderstanding as well as truths about life throughout this book.

What are truths about life? I take the premise that there is meaning and purpose in each person's life. The exercises in this text will help you uncover the deeper significance of your existence. I invite you to explore the healthy usefulness of all the advice we get. My intention is not to give advice, but to help you explore how to apply what we receive into useful tools to create joy and belonging (both in the relationship with the self and others). Unlike asking you to accept advice, guidance, or techniques, the words here invite you to reveal the truth that is already living in you.

Since all individuals exist in reality as part of the living collective, we have relationships with one other. The journey of this book is to discover how to create and sustain meaningful connections that enrich your life.

Sincerely,

Suna Senman

The One

Take care of the one first.
Inner peace is the beginning.
Make peace between body and soul.

Nourish both.
Allow for healing in both
When accidents happen
And wounds are inflicted.

Create a routine that cares for both daily.
Feed the soul first
With scripture, prayer, and meditation,
Then, feed the body
With fresh raw food and protein
Like an almond butter toast with berries.

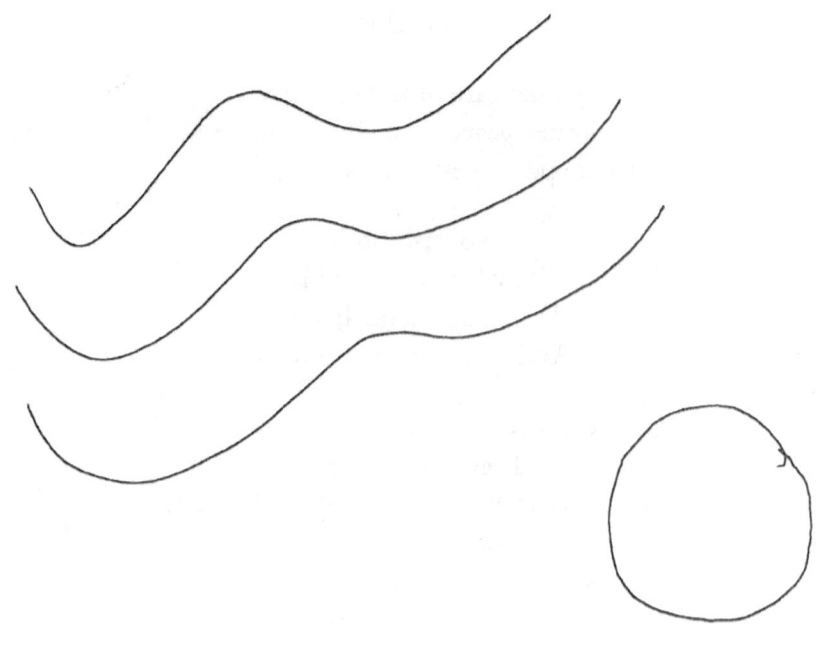

THE
BEGINNING

The Beginning

Peace is the second book in a trilogy. The first volume is *Being*. The third manuscript is *Full*. Together the three are *Being, Peace, Full*. We know so much about wisdom, yet many of us are in a process (some call it a journey) toward becoming full of peace. If enough people become interested, those individuals who make efforts to be full of peace can gather into a community of peacefulness.

As with the first book, *Being*, *Peace* is an exploration—a journey that I decided to take to manifest peace in my own self with an invitation for others to join me. I have received wisdom and guidance from many mentors. Ultimately, at the core of each relationship is the universal truth speaking to me. My task is to perfect my listening so that I can hear its message. Then not only do I want to hear, I want to become. "Becoming" means that I have to stop the cycles of all the dynamics that prevent me from being peaceful.

What is being peaceful?

Peace actions are actions that counter the violent actions in the world. Both actions require your energy, but peace actions may seem more difficult to create than violent actions. Redirecting energy from old habits that contribute to violence into actions that bring greater love and respect is the method of being peaceful.

What are violent actions?

Any action that violates the respect and integrity of another being is a violent action. A violent action can be physical, verbal, mental, or emotional.

Because the only control a person has is over his or her own thoughts and actions, the focus of this book is about how one person can create thoughts, words, and actions of peace. The more people who make this individual effort, the larger the realm of peace can become. The thoughts, words, and actions of peace are not necessarily equivalent to pacifism. They are consciously active decisions. From the best of my understanding with all the knowledge that I have now, I choose to think, speak, and act respectfully. Bringing peace does

3

not necessarily mean being liked, either. Martin Luther King, Jr., as a great peacemaker, was strongly disliked by many.

Being nice is not equivalent to being a peacemaker. When a mother squeezes her toddler's jaw and pulls him away from the child he is biting, does the toddler feel his mother is being nice to him? When the parent will not give the teen girl permission to go to a dance club, does the girl think her parent is nice? Was Jesus being nice when he spoke to Peter and said "Get behind me Satan"? Did Peter feel that Jesus was being nice to him? Things happen in the world that require not-so-nice responses in order to move toward peace and goodness.

Therefore being a maker of peace is not always a good feeling. A maker of peace does not necessarily look special or become popular. Why would a person choose to be a maker of peace? The contrary contributes to an environment that ultimately makes us miserably fearful. The choice is still ours to make. Each one of us can choose to be makers of peace or contributors to violence. There is no in-between. We may make choices unconsciously and we may make choices consciously. You, as the reader, make your choice, too. This book is a journey to discover how to be a peacemaker.

Let's introduce ourselves as we begin this journey. Please introduce yourself:

Name:

What is the meaning of your name?

Where have you lived?

Where do you live now?

What languages or dialects do you speak?

What is your family background?

How many siblings do you have and what is your position in the birth order?

What are your family traditions?

What are your closest relationships?

What are your favorite things to do?

How do you spend your days?

What are the five most important things to you? (Prioritize, if possible)
1.
2.
3.
4.
5.

This is a good beginning introduction for the journey of our relationship.

<u>Our first steps together</u>:

- Why do you want to write this book with me?
- What lead you to this point?
- What attracted you to this project?

You can write your thoughts either before or after you read my reasons for wanting to write this book with you (see next page).

My reason for writing this book with you:

I felt as if I stood on a mountaintop at the podium in the library where I spoke about my first book, *Being*. My intent, as I embarked on writing those words, was to be as honest and raw open as possible—revealing my being and also recording a reminder of inner truths to myself. The talk at the library was another exposure of my naked soul in spoken form to a small audience and a camera. I was afraid of being in the spotlight in my vulnerable state. Will people take my good intentions and judge my imperfections? Will they value the pearls of my heart or spill and trample them on the ground? The unknown was scary. Yet, I knew that in order to grow, I had to empty myself.

From that peak, I felt myself look at the long trip down the slope to the beginning of a new journey upward—the journey to peace. I asked myself these questions:

How do I find peace?
Do I create peace?
Does peace find me?
Is peace a natural inheritance?

This book is my journey in the quest to find answers.

Understanding that my experience is my reality, I asked myself, "Can my experience be peace?" My answer is that I believe so. I believe that regardless of the situation, *I can maintain an environment of peace through the power of the heart.* I challenge myself with living the truth that Jesus spoke in his words, "…it is not what goes into the mouth that defiles a person, but what comes out of the mouth; this defiles a person" (Matthew 15:11). The opposite must be true—what I express can create the peace for which I yearn. This is a frightening challenge, since I know that I have failed to produce complete peace in the past. Yet, the present is a new blank page reaching toward a future that both builds upon and remedies the past. As I embark on this journey, I grant myself forgiveness in advance for any flaw or mistake I make in the process of learning to be a manifestation of peace.

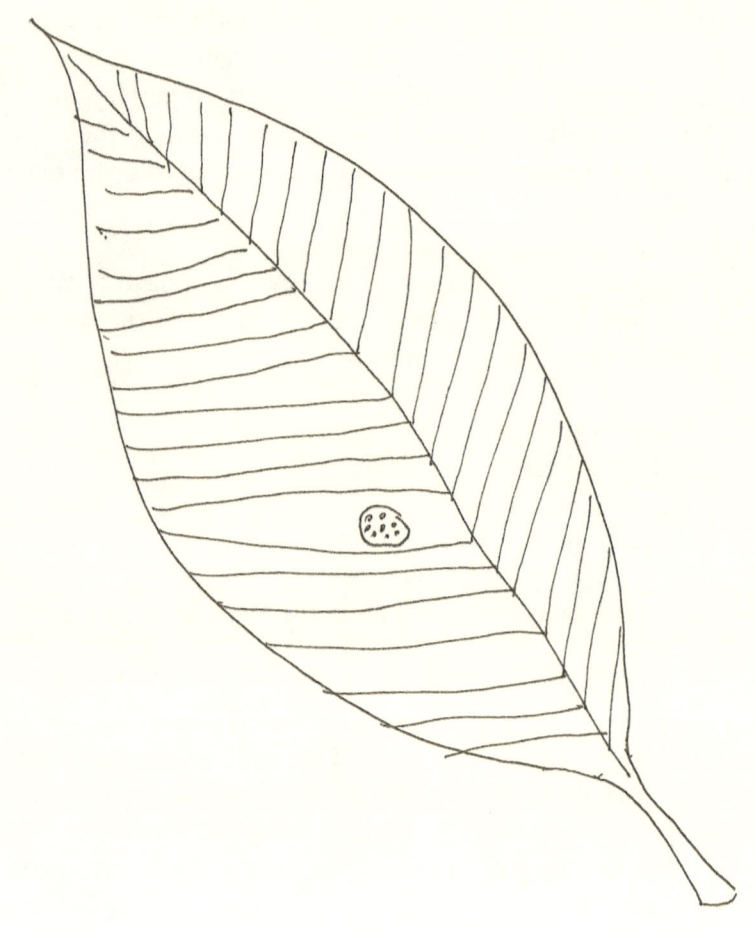

PEACE

Peace (one)

I
I am
I am breathing
I am breathing in
I am breathing in fresh air
I am breathing in fresh air to nourish
I am breathing in fresh air to nourish my body
I am breathing in fresh air to nourish my body and soul

I
I am
I am breathing
I am breathing out
I am breathing out expired elements
I am breathing out expired elements once useful
I am breathing out expired elements once useful—no longer needed
I am breathing out expired elements once useful—no longer needed to let go

I
I create
I create space
I create space for new
I create space for new good
I create space for new, good experiences
I create space for new, good experiences with each breath
I create space for new, good experiences with each breath in
I create space for new, good experiences with each breath in faith
I create space for new, good experiences with each breath in faith and love

I
I create
I create good
I create good substance
I create good substance with each breath
I create good substance with each breath out
I create good substance with each breath out in acts
I create good substance with each breath out in acts of love
I create good substance with each breath out in acts of love and faith
I create good substance with each breath out in acts of love and faith-making Peace

First, we need to define peace.

I believe that peace, love, and happiness are a package. I would like to ask you to define peace, too. Try to write something more descriptive than "the absence of conflict, war, and strife."

What does peace mean to you?

My definition of Peace:

- Peace is harmonizing contrasting elements.
- Peace is having sight of possibility—possibility that births hope.
- Peace is responding to the needs of others with love—not always with action but always with love.
- Peace is respecting and valuing life.
- Peace is about resonating with universal truths and absolute values—beyond our images, assumptions, or internalized objects that we associate with the first cause that has many names: God, Source, Higher Self, Allah, Great Wisdom, Jehovah, etc.
- Peace is light and space for more light.

Building Peace

As I think about building a world of peace, I question what peace actually is. For instance, if I thought about designing and building a house (an exercise that I actually did), I would need to have an idea of the general structure and of every aspect of that house down to the annoying details in order for the house to materialize. Because I truly want to build a world of peace, not just talk about one, I need to look at constructing peace as tediously as I pursued manifesting a house.

I believe that it is important to clearly define peace in order to know what we are trying to build. In constructing a house, a builder recognizes several divisions of labor: laying the foundation, framing, plumbing, electrical work, landscaping, roofing, painting, etc. I have identified thirteen areas that I consider aspects of peace and have named and organized the chapters of this book accordingly. The aspects of peace are: honesty, relationships, work-sweat, dreaming, beauty, truth, love, value, compassion, justice, responsibility, happiness, and new peace being. Another person may choose different words to define the characteristics of peace. As long as people agree on the core concepts of the attributes of peace, they can build it together. Perhaps only those who can collaborate around basic core concepts will create and live in the world of peace and the others will live outside—like one group building a community (or castle) together and others not wanting to be part of that community. If a person wants to join the community once it is built, they will need to adapt to the core concepts of peace to live there. If the peace community accepts other concepts, it becomes a different community.

Core concepts are different than unique expressions of ideas. Core concepts are universal and unchanging, whereas, unique expressions of ideas can be either individual or cultural interpretations of core concepts. For example, there are many different cultural traditions around basic rights of passage such as accepting a new person into the community (i.e. baptism or circumcision, confirmation or bar mitzvah), marriage, and death. These expressions have different nuances to the core meaningfulness of life changes.

The unique expressions such as white wedding gowns, flower filled halls, vows, eulogies, sprinkling with water, or scarring the skin are all unique expressions as interpretations of a core concept. A core concept of peace would be respect. A unique expression of respect might be bowing in the East or hand-shakes in the West. While each culture has a different expression, the core peace concepts of value and respect are commonly accepted.

I choose to act from a mindful connection with the core of my being, with respect for those around me.

Even within the American culture, there are subcultures for expressing respect. In the South, you can respectfully state the blunt truth if you add, "Bless your heart." You can say, "Bless your heart, sweetie, I think you're making a mistake." Or "Bless his heart, he forgot to take the garbage out and the hole house stinks." In New York, the phrase is, "With all due respect." You can say, "With all due respect, I disagree with your ideas." These phrases confirm respect prior to expressing contrast or conflict. Life is full of contrast and conflict, yet you can create peace and harmony when you honor each person. You can express your honest perspectives no matter how contradictory they seem while maintaining the dignity of all involved. However you speak your thoughts, if they are conveyed with respect, you can be received.

HONESTY

My Honest Inner-Dialogue

I have to be sharp
I want to show compassion to my suffering friend
I want my body fit and energetic
I have gotta be on time
Today I have to get in a ninety-minute workout, take an hour to
get ready, get breakfast by 11:00, leave between 11:15 and 11:30
My prayers have to be sincere
I have gotta follow up

STOP

Honestly,
I am sluggish
I can not concentrate
My prayers drift into cartoon thoughts
I feel fat and like a blob
My body's not moving out of this bed now
I can stop

...
...
...

It feels good to breathe

OH, Look!
I am rolling out of bed!

Honesty

What is honesty?

Accepting reality without interpretation or escape is being honest. Sometimes, we reject or "reform" reality when the honest reality is too painful. So, in order to accept reality, we have to endure all emotional experiences that accompany all situations in our lives; both the painful and the joyful. Honesty is full acceptance of your being and your environment. (Refer to the first book *Being* in order to understand honesty more fully.)

Take a moment to meditate on these questions as I am reflecting, too:

- What does honesty have to do with peace?
- What does honesty have to do with any element of peace like respect or happiness?

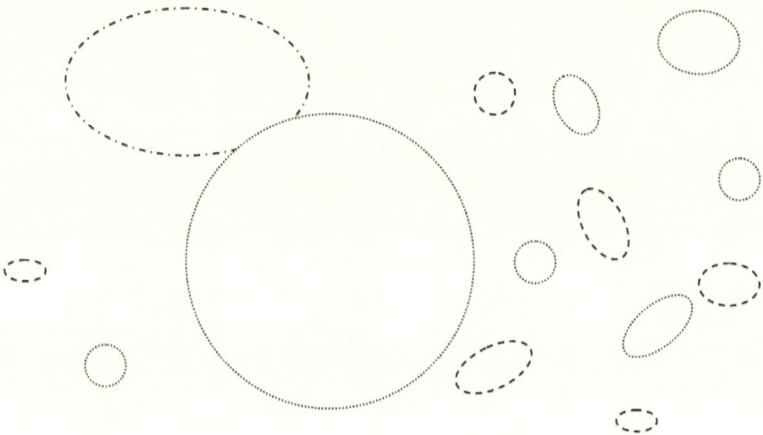

Honesty is simply accepting "what is" without judgment; you accept what you are experiencing (feeling, seeing, hearing, or thinking) without opinion. Redefining one thing to become another is not honesty. Renaming feelings to be facts; or assuming what you see to be what another person thinks; or believing what you hear is what you know are all ways of escaping reality and the opposite of truthfulness. Redefining is a very common practice with a lot of people. Recognizing honesty versus reframing experiences may be a challenging concept to comprehend. The reinterpretation of direct experience into an altered "truth" is often at the root of conflict. Sometimes creative thoughts manifest assumptions that replace honest fact.

Create your own picture of Relationships here

RELATIONSHIPS

Life is partly what we make of it
And partly what was is made
By the friends we choose.

—*Tennessee Williams*

Realm bEtween Space and Time

Women are married to Fathers and Sons
Their true spouses are
Locked behind doors of
Conscious thought

Men live with Daughters and Mothers
Their children are orphans
Looking for parents

No man to trust
Because my mind can not be trusted
Tell me—
Tell me
What to do

Lost on the line of time

Building Peace Relationships

These are the elements for building a true relationship:

Trust (Security)
Gratitude
Direction

Like a flowering plant or any growing thing, a healthy relationship has these three aspects: trust, gratitude, and direction. Trust is the root of a true relationship. Gratitude is the stem that grows the relationship longer. Direction is the action that moves the relationships into growth and stability.

Trust is the absolute fundamental seed of a relationship. Faith in the other is the genesis of a true connection. Prior to trustworthiness, the link between people seems to be more an activity of curiosity and attraction—a motivation to bond. Yet the interactions around magnetism are not more than a potential for a friendship. People simply recognize that the other exists in time and space, and this "other" affects me. Yet, only when dependability is established does a secure tie form. Then on the foundation of the steadiness and security, each experience together forms a memory like a growing stem coming forth from the seed. Trust is the unseen, under the ground seed and DNA of the alliance.

Each seed has a different DNA. Each relationship is different. There are parental associations with parents, mentors, and authorities. There is trust in different areas on different levels. Reliability within a parental relationship is the knowledge that they support you. Confidence with mentors is that they guide you. Trust in authorities is that they ensure fairness. These characteristics are the different qualities in parent type relationships. Then there are many peer relationships, too, from personal to business.

Let's look at the seeds of our relationship, trust. What is your confidence in me? What is my faith in you?

Your belief in me will be based on:

- ✓ How my words resonate with your inner truth;
- ✓ What you know about me;
- ✓ What relationships I have created; and
- ✓ The fruits of my partnerships and how they appeal to you.

I am fortunate to have several good friends founded in honesty and trust. Some friendships have endured for over thirty years, others have developed over the past ten years, and some are newly forming. Honesty and trustworthiness are the nourishing fertilizers for the root of our relationship. We have stability in our trust even if we disagree or disappoint one another. Disappointments that are recognized with sincerity can be overcome. Breaches in trust eat at the root of the relationship and eventually wither the bond.

I have a friend whose alcoholism and dementia have progressed to the extent that she can no longer live alone or take care of herself. Yet, she feels that she is caring for herself and others. When I first met her, she was funny, had many colorful stories, and we enjoyed very good times together. After noticing some bizarre behavior and meeting some of her old friends, I learned that she was in denial of her alcoholism and her medical health condition. My friendship turned into a confused mix of friend and caretaker. Because of her denial, I couldn't gauge if she was being truthful or not. I recognize that her conscious intention was to be loving and caring, yet, I was watching her put many people into very uncomfortable situations, including me. The structure of our relationship became unstable as the foundation of trust crumbled. I am not fully relaxed or comfortable meeting with her anymore, knowing that she hides information. The roots of our relationship were a mix of life-watering support (caring for one another) and toxic distrust. The viability of the relationship depends on the continuation or cessation of the mistrust.

Gratitude is the attitude of respect that grows the connection and pulls forth the trust through the core of the association. Every experience becomes like a building block or another ring of growth on the relationship. The relationship deepens and develops. *Gratitude keeps the relationship growing in true love*—like following the direction of the sun. Gratitude is the perspective taken toward the other person, their words and their actions. Just being grateful for the other person's existence is like breathing. Then their words and actions become bonuses.

I am thankful that I have friends with whom I can share my concerns, my plans and accomplishments. I appreciate the care I get from their phone calls, get-togethers, and nurturing acts.

I show my gratitude in regular communication in order to grow those relationships. Communications can be short e-mails, phone calls, a note, little gifts, or even a prayer or sending a good thought. Little gifts are simple acts like picking up a friend's child from school when needed, picking up her favorite tea when I am at the grocery, giving a quick call, or giving a compliment. Great friendships are built on moments of good interactions.

List the people for whose simple existence you are grateful. Then take note of some simple little things you did to grow your relationships recently:

Person	Action

Direction is the growth hormone insuring that a relationship exists in a perpetual sustainability, from now to now to now. Any relationship that is not actively in the growth process is in the dying process. When people settle and think, "This is a good relationship. Let's not change," they have entered the dying phase of the relationship. There must be direction and motivation to grow. There is no "staying the same" in life. Life is constant change; more change is growth and less change is atrophy. Pay attention to your muscles— relationships need exercise too.

Simple things like communicating, giving a hug, spending time together, and thinking positive thoughts about the person grow a relationship. Different actions serve different types of relationships. Relationships also change and grow. For example, the relationship a mother has with her three-year-old daughter grows into another type of relationship with the same daughter at twelve years old and later at eighteen years old. Also the relationship between friends can grow and change into business partnerships or other life partnerships. Some actions are more appropriate than others in these specific relationships. Yet, often we forget to feed the relationships with enough of gestures that keep them healthy. Every now and then we need to take inventory to notice if we are feeding our relationships toward healthy growth. (Do not forget the relationship that you have with yourself! Refer back to *Being: A Process*, the first book in this trilogy, in order to understand the relationship with the self more fully.) Take note of some simple little things you did to grow your relationships recently.

List three or more relationships you have and the direction that you wish for them to go:

Relationship	Direction

The vibrant heart
forgives.
This living heart
is the core of true self -
eternal
This heart
Is not in your image of self,
or
The self you want to become
It is not in
Your airbrushed pictures
or the expression on your face
to make you look "politically correct"
or intellectually fashionable

Value and virtue
are
within
you.
You
Exist
In the origin of
being.
As there are many different trees
rooted
in the same earth,
Each unique human is
rooted
in the same origin.

The origin is
home.
Home
Is in the heart
of
The origin.
As the original parent
Of life,
The first heartbeat that longed
To create life
And did
From darkness
To life

The origin
lives
in your heart
as the first heartbeat continuing
to turn darkness
into life.

Peace in relationships with flexibility:

Respect yourself and respect others. You have needs, and you create healthy habits for yourself. You are a unique individual with your distinctive needs. Others have their needs and habits. As peers, we need to respect each other's choices. As parents, the matter is more complex, because we are taking responsibility for dependent children. We have the right to ask others to respect our needs, but do not have the right to ask others to change themselves simply because we think that they should be different. Respect others for who they are and respect yourself for who you are. You can harmonize your different ways. As two different cultures collide, each is asked to adjust for harmony.

Routine and variation are both important in order to keep balance in a person's life. Each person has their routines that include self-care and caring for their environment. These routines are as unique to individuals as fingerprints. In families, routines are similar, yet as children grow into adults, they individuate and develop their own routines and styles. Variation creates space for growth. Changing up a routine in different times or situations allows for new experiences and self-development. Routine is like an anchor; variation is like an explorer's boat.

Examples of routines that I have in my life are

- As I wake, doing a "check-in" with my being, then aligning and attuning with the Source energy through meditation or prayer;
- Putting on my gym clothes immediately as I get up in order to get my workout done before other activities take over the day; and
- Making my bed within ten minutes of getting out of it.

Examples of changing up my routine are

- Writing down dreams as I wake and allowing my inner

being to express itself instead of meditating. The dreams are wisdom from my true self that guide me;

- Instead of immediately working out at the gym, I get on calls to Europe (and sometimes stretch on my floor while I talk). The opportunities to connect to my overseas relationships enhance my being. My muscles require days of rest, too; and
- I always make my bed within ten minutes of getting up, yet when I change the sheets, the process takes longer.

My routine may seem odd to someone else. Each person develops their routine and style of managing in a way that seems to make their life run most smoothly, yet another person may look at that routine and think it can be improved. We create peace when we respect other people's unique ways of functioning. A parent, in particular, can carry his or her responsibilities of teaching routines and healthy life styles beyond "the expiration date."

As humans, we often have to stop ourselves from wanting to change another person. People often want to help others. But beware of offering unsolicited correction as it often steps over the boundaries of the other person's integrity. Unsolicited guidance usually stems from a desire to parent ourselves, to correct and improve ourselves.

Please share examples and experiences of routines from your life:

Peace in relationships: Attachment-Detachment

In order to explain the balance of "you-me-us" concepts, we need to be mindful of schemas. Schemas are the emotional and experiential attachments we have to words or objects. For example, "attachment" may stimulate a feeling of sticky confinement or it may generate an image of an adoring, cherishing mother-infant bond. Those two schemas are very different. So when a person with one schema talks about attachment with a person with the other schema, misunderstanding and conflict occurs. Therefore, it is important to listen beyond words—to listen to the heart. Both schemas exist and are acceptable, but hearing the intention of the conveyor of a message—listening to the heart—is where understanding is created.

Hearing the heart of a person provides a mindfulness of reality. A good therapist listens to the heart beneath the words. People often say one thing but mean another, as if they are leaving clues or simultaneously want to be heard and not heard. What do people really want? We all want to express truth, love, and beauty so that it is received and reflected back to us. Sometimes people want to express lies, hurt, and ugliness, because that's what they have seen. They both want and do not want to see that reflected back. The experience of lies, hurt, and ugliness is unpleasant. And yet, a person wants to be seen. If a person has allowed lies, hurt, and ugliness to penetrate their being, these factors becomes part of their being that they need to express. He or she will continue to express everything that is in them—a mix of lies, hurt, and ugliness along with the truth, love, and beauty of his or her original, natural state. These contradictory qualities coexist until the person cleans house and lets go of the garbage. Because we always express what is inside of us, it is also the mix that will be reflected back. We see what is inside. Therefore, when a person sees jealousy, greed, gluttony, or any of the "sins" in others, the wise person will recognize that there are at least crumbs of those things inside him- or herself.

Attachment and detachment are key concepts to understand in order to navigate the complicated "mix." If you can clean house often (even several times a day), you practice healthy attachment and detachment. If you are mindful of the things that approach you through the day and are discerning of their core (love or ugliness), then you can let go of the unwanted ugliness quickly so that you can practice filling yourself with truth, love, and beauty.

Some people love playing in ugly messes. When I have tried to engage people in expressions of truth, love, and beauty, they are often eager to engage, yet, unwilling to let go of ugliness. Some people get attached to the concept of "ownership." A person felt that she owned me and tried to prevent me from expressing a part of myself that evoked a feeling of dishonesty in her. She had talked herself into believing that her lifestyle was beautiful, but my expression of truth triggered a realization that she contained ugliness. Her reaction was to discredit me and push me away instead of doing some "housecleaning" or making her own necessary changes. She was afraid of change. In her ownership attitude of me as her friend, she insisted that I do not speak about some of my ideas. What she tried to own slipped away. *I detached from her instead of detaching from a part of a truth of my being.*

Socialization of children in many current schools includes a process of requiring them to detach from a part of their truth in order to conform to a communal standard. The truth is what a child is interested in. The imposed standard is what the community says a child should be interested in. For example, a child may be fascinated with stacking stones and building. The community forces an agenda that this child needs to read and study toward becoming a lawyer. The truth in the child is to engage in the art and occupation of building with his hands. The child may retain the truth against the pressures of the community and be called a failure, or he may be worn down by the community's persistence to deny his truth and take the garbage of living up to someone else's expectation, thereby creating an unhealthy attachment. The garbage will continue to rot inside while he makes appearances to be successful. His own inner truth will persist. He will continue be a "mix" until he cleans house. For him, housecleaning will be liberating as he lets go of the garbage and thrives in his own truth. To others, the housekeeping may look like he's throwing away his investment, though some may recognize that he is in the process of becoming his true self.

Healthy attachment and detachment in relationships is a clarification of "you, me, and us." We strive to achieve to greater love, truth, and beauty through each other. Sometimes a person does not want to let go of their garbage, but wants you to carry it with them, too. Maybe they want you to carry their garbage for them (passive-aggressive projection). Unfortunately, I have had the experience of some people who attribute their garbage to me and convince themselves that I am their garbage. These few people are severely detached from reality, but because of attractive façades, they exist in society as "successful" people.

Complete the internal inventory below (continue on the next page if necessary).

Garbage	Love, Truth, Beauty

Relationship breaches

Expectations make disappointments possible. When there are no expectations, there is nothing to be disappointed over. Some expectations are spelled out clearly in contracts. And still the parties involved can interpret contracts differently. Varied interpretations lead to divergent expectations.

When expectations are countered by contradictory behavior, disappointments occur and can break trust in relationships.

Think about a disappointment you had with someone. What was your expectation? How did he or she breach your expectation?

My most immediate breach of expectation is an experience I just had with my little six-pound dog. We have a routine of getting out of bed in the morning and going out for her morning potty. She usually walks to the door with me and sits while I put on my coat and boots, before putting on her jacket and leash. This morning she started to follow me to the stairs, but then squatted outside the bedroom door to pee on the carpet. I was *hugely* upset; I picked her up and shut her in the bathroom while I grabbed paper towel and cleaner and cleaned up the mess. I continued to carry both her and my disappointment as I brought the soiled paper towels to the garbage waiting at the street (to be picked up this morning). I carried my irritation out to the middle of the yard where I set her down to empty anything left in her bladder. She just stood there, frozen like a statue. I realized then that our relationship was disturbed. She was feeling bad about herself that she disappointed me and I felt imbalanced that I was carrying this heavy frustration. I crouched down, picked her up, looked her in the eyes, and expressed myself. I told her about my expectation and displeasure and I told her that I love her. I needed to voice my anticipations where I could hear them, too. As I looked at her, I could readjust my hopes to realize that she's still a puppy. I need to continue to carry her to the door if I want to be certain that her first bladder release of the morning does not occur on my carpet. (Or accept that I'll be replacing the carpet.) I could drop my heavy discontent and begin healing the broken relationship. We could move forward with our normal routine.

What heavy disappointments do you need to drop?

Let me also explain how the rest of the day went with my canine relationship:

Although I decided to drop the disappointment, my little puppy continued to be a puppy; she wet on the wood floor twice and pooped once. Even though I have newspapers on the floor, she does not live up to my expectation of relieving herself on the papers. I believe she has expectations of me as well. She probably wants me to take her out when she needs to relieve herself. My puppy and I have communication difficulties. She does not seem to know what I want and I do not know what she wants. Even though I decided to drop my disappointment and lower my expectations, I need to continue to make efforts to improve communication. Both my puppy and I want to make one another happy.

Just like dogs have different communication styles, people also have various expressive approaches. Learning a person's communication style gives you the opportunity to read his or her expectations and to communicate yours effectively. A person who is very "net" wants just the facts and may not understand metaphor or inferential language. Some people are very sensitive to facial expressions and body language, so they will "hear" more than your words. Others have internal dialogues running while you speak so that your words are filtered and twisted into other meanings. If your style is different than the person with whom you want to communicate, you probably need to make adjustments in the way you listen and express yourself.

Love and Fear

Although life is based on relationships, there is a difference between polarities (supportive of creativity) and dualities (counteractive pairs). Love and fear, for example, are dualities that counteract one another. Love is diminished by fear and vice versa. Even though the two may appear to be complimentary, they contradict one another and produce nothing. Worry is a love and fear duality—hoping for a positive outcome (love) and visualizing a negative outcome (fear). One negates the other. They are antithetical to one another. They produce nothing.

True polarities of life produce more life and are

- Positive and negative charges;
- Creation (building) and destruction (letting go so that space for new can exist);
- Giving and receiving; and
- Object and space (no object).

Polarities are life-producing relationships, while dualities negate life.

Some philosophies create confusion by categorizing certain polarities as dualities. For example, "the spirit and the flesh" is a confusing categorization of the body fighting against the soul. The Creator manifested both the heavens and the earth (the spirit and the body) to function together in order to multiply more of the good that He created. Perhaps the more sincere expression of duality that those philosophies wish to express is the fear of physical death vs. the fear of spiritual death.

The word "fear" holds different schemas (or attachments). One schema is raw fear, as in a pure emotion. Fear as a pure emotion (like the feeling you experience when you almost hit another car while driving) is healthy. Fear is a natural emotion. Emotions are like senses. They help us become aware of our situation so that we have necessary information to make decisions. Fear, anger, sadness, happiness, and confusion are all emotions that give us healthy feedback about our environment.

Thoughts can trigger emotions just like thinking about chocolate cake can make your mouth water. A memory can evoke feelings as if the event is really happening. When thoughts and imagination about a situation trigger fear, you will experience the same "danger, do not go there" feeling as when you almost hit another car. The thoughts feel like reality, but are not always linked to reality. The fearful thoughts will often keep you from truly exploring whatever you are thinking about. For example, if you were told that touching your genitals will make God angry, then you have a fear thought that prevents you from exploring a part of your body. When you want to use that part of your body to create children, the fear-based thought may continue to say "do not go there." A subconscious, contrasting force meets your desire. You can feel guilty for having your innate, human desire as your fear-based thought speaks. Until you uncover your subconscious (or conscious) thoughts and align them with truthfulness, you may feel a frustration that you could call "bad luck."

Where emotionally charged thoughts exist, truth and love may be inhibited, though they can never be annihilated. *Emotionally charged thoughts are often the fruits of over-thinking a situation.* Our creativity can go beyond the boundaries of reality. We can engage in over-creation, just like processing food to the point where living nutrients are killed. The thoughts that we create in excess of natural situations become disharmonious with life. Actually, the emotionally charged thought "creation" is not really a creation at all, but a distortion of the natural situation. In order to support life, identify emotionally charged thoughts and dissolve them. Instead of allowing the unknown to become a fearful thought, place love and light in its place. Love eliminates fears like light dissolves darkness. A simple exercise in breathing can identify fear (pain or physical fear, mental, and/or emotional fear) and place love and light in its place. Other emotionally charged thoughts can distort truth and healthy life.

I confess, I know about emotionally charged thoughts from my own practice of over-thinking. I regularly practice the exercise of identifying and dissolving often.

Complete the following exercise in dissolving emotionally charged thoughts:

1) Identify thought
2) Reduce thought to the bare facts
3) Identify raw emotion (Fear, anger, sadness, joy, confusion)
4) Breathe

Thoughts	Facts	Emotion

BREATHE
Love
Light

Peace work

S.W.E.A.T.:

1) Stillness
2) Work
3) Everything
4) Answers
5) Toughness or resilience

Stillness:

Stillness is the starting point—take the time to find out where you are now. The "where you are" is not a physical location. It is a spiritual location—where is your awareness? Where is your gratitude? Where is your focus? You are either creating peace or disrupting peace. Regardless of what is occurring around you, within you is your creative force going in one direction or another. While you may not be in full control of what occurs around you, you are in control of what comes from within you. The external environment may tempt you to conform, but you decide your direction at all times. The external environment may pull you physically in a direction where you do not wish to go, but the internal direction is still in your control. Viktor Frankl illustrates this point in his written account of his experiences in a concentration camp, *Man's Search for Meaning*, Peace, therefore, is attainable at anytime in any place. If you know where you are, you can begin to move toward Peace and even live in the territory of Peace.

Work:

Work is effort designed to bring a fruitful result. It takes work to till soil and plant seeds. If the effort put into tilling the soil created good ground for the seed, and the seed came from the plant you wish to reproduce, you should have a good crop. The problem lies in preparing the soil (the situation) and discerning which seeds to plant (deciding what outcome you want and recognizing the starting point for your desired end result).

To find the right seed, look carefully at the tree from which tree it comes. For example, if you want to make a good income in order to have a house and car like the Joneses, ask yourself from what tree of desire does that seed come. Comparing yourself to another person is like determining where you are in the ocean by seeing how far you stand from the person in the boat with you. You have no real idea where you are—only that you are in a boat with someone else. You might be headed for rapids or a waterfall or perhaps you are just floating in circles. You may feel comforted by the company, but when you realize that you're both lost or in trouble, you may find yourself feeling alone and desperate.

The seed of desire that comes from wanting to look like or be like someone else (even if these messages come from mass media) will grow a plant desiring to be something other than itself. You, or the plant, are then living in a false reality. My advice to young people looking for colleges, careers, and occupations in life is to find the still quiet place inside and listen, then dare to act on what you heard from a sincere place inside, without following distractions. I remind myself to always check inside, accept who I am, look at where I am, and keep heading in the direction of my sincere heart's desire. This method keeps me planting good seeds that are not "genetically altered" from the original good source.

Even with conscious effort to identify and plant good seeds, we sometimes discover that our effort is not producing good results. Do not force it. Ask yourself what kind of result you are getting from your input? Measure the value of your actions by your results. If you are putting more effort in than what you get back, you are creating an imbalance. You might be putting your effort into matters that you have no business getting involved in

Putting energy in places you do not belong is like giving unsolicited advice. Giving advice when it is not asked for is a waste of time and energy that could have been used elsewhere more productively. Can you think of a situation you've had (or are having now) that does not seem to work? Writing about it will produce clarity.

Share your experience here.

Below I also write about my situation that didn't work:

I met a woman who became a good friend with whom I spent a lot of time every week for the past few years. She had a lovely, giving personality and complained of going through a tough time when we met. I noticed after a while that her "tough time" was a constant condition of not being able to pay her bills and needing loans. As the relationship became more draining on my resources (time and energy included), I had to drop the unbalanced relationship. I still recognize her love and charm, yet the dynamic of helping her get out of a tough time wasn't working. I now recognize her situation as chronic, and I limit my help.

I did my best to help this friend for years only to find that I had fallen into a trap of fruitless effort. My perspective is that of the foot soldier on the battlefield. I see only what is right in front of me. I watch my steps as I see the ground at my feet. Yet, I do not see what's around the corner or 100 feet down the road. The general on the mountaintop sees the whole field and directs His soldiers to safety and success. When I set my awareness to the higher consciousness in meditation and prayer, I get a glimpse from the mountaintop. Direction that I feel or hear from the higher conscious sometimes conflicts with my own logical thinking. This is where faith comes in. It allows me to take action in accordance with the Higher Consciousness even against my own present understanding. Additionally, I do not always have the clarity to distinguish between the situations I wish to see versus the real situation—reality. I bought into my friend's illusion until I gained more information and a more accurate perspective. My understanding is constantly expanding as I follow the greater consciousness rather than my own simple thought process.

Everything:

Reality exists as well as all the interpretations and illusions that humans add to their reality. Interpretations and illusions comprise "everything." Reality comes primarily from the source of life, the *I am*. Reality is the set of principles that govern life—the things that affect us whether or not we believe in them. These principles rule our physical and spiritual existence. My interpretations of how these principles function may be distorted or incomplete. My interpretations become my belief. My belief (in my distorted understandings of reality) will be challenged in my life when things aren't working out. I can either correct my beliefs or create illusions so that my distorted understanding of reality can fit in. My everything (both the reality I live in and my beliefs) guides my life.

Doubting the existence of my Source and distractions from my core being are two things that get me off balance.

The first obstacle is doubting the existence of the Source:

Belief in the Supreme Force is each individual's personal responsibility. The Force goes by many names: Higher Power, Heavenly Parent, God, Allah, Jehovah, Holy Spirit, Divine Force, the Great Mystery, and the Source, among others. We have to have many names because the Force is so great that it is beyond the confinement of a single name. Most often, the issue is not that our belief is absent, but that our belief needs to constantly grow. Like getting to know a friend—even one you've known for years—each interaction gives you greater knowledge of that person. The key is to engage in the relationship with that friend, or with the Higher Power in this case, in order to know it and develop greater trust and friendship.

If you center only on yourself (your own wishes, feelings, desires, and experience), then you have no space to allow for your friend to connect to you. You act like a small child toward a parent. The child has no interest in the parent other than what the parent can do for it: feed it, change it, and comfort it. Like a small child, you get angry at the parent for not giving you the candy you want now. You depend on the parent and resent the parent at the same time. You think, *I want to make up my own mind. I do not want to be controlled by that overbearing authority. I want to do things my way.* As a parent allows a small child to do things his or her way, the child loses a sense of direction, loses control, and gets into situations that he/she has no ability to recover from alone. He or she needs to be rescued. Like a small child wandering into a crowd, into the street, off into the woods, or even toward an electric socket, the child does not know how to protect his or her life, much less know where to go for greater happiness and success.

Security, happiness, and success come through a process of relating to the Higher Power. Maturing as a human being brings you to a place of believing in the Higher Power and understanding that the greatest need in your life is to continually develop your relationship with it. You will never be at a place where you do not need that Higher Power first. Just as the more you know, the more you realize that you do not know, the more you know God's wisdom, the more you realize that you need God's wisdom. The challenge is to get beyond the initial ignorance.

Write about your relationship with your Higher Power (or whatever name you use):

<u>The second obstacle is distraction.</u>

Many things look worthwhile, yet on this earth we have limited time and space to sort out what we feel is worthwhile and what is not. Simply sit and listen to the wisdom in your heart. Just like with anything, we can only see the fruits of listening to our hearts when we actually take time to do it. Then we need to take action based on our understanding. Yet as we move out into the world, there are many distractions that pull us off course from our original direction. We find a clear direction and gain understanding from our silent time. Then we step into the world with intentions to act, but are immediately confronted with something else that masks itself as worthwhile. We can dance with that attraction or politely say, "I wish you well," and continue on the way toward our original goal.

Sometimes that worthwhile thing is a part of the goal and you can walk together. When the worthwhile thing says, "Let's go over here now—come my way," and takes you away from the original path (which will bring you into a deeper connection with your true self and your Source or God), then the worthwhile thing becomes a distraction.

In order to help identify your distractions, list your activities and goals. First list your largest life goals:

1)
2)
3)

Now list your activities and the goal they fall under. Those things that do not lead you to the largest goals could be distractions, even though they lead to other goals.

ACTIVITY	GOAL

When you work against your own inner direction, you wear yourself out. You can try to travel with someone or something going in a tangential direction to your own true longing for a while. At some point, the stress of the reaching for someone else's direction becomes too much and the bond needs to break or you will find yourself off course. After breaking the bond, simply connecting in discussion with a person who relates to your true direction can give life and energy. Then every little interaction with truth strengthens you.

When you find your right place and direction, you do not need to give energy to correcting problems that are outside of your domain. Your time and energy are valuable; invest them into the things for which your heart longs. When you invest in your right direction, it feels like having survived a riptide. Now you can flow with the tide that sets you back on safe ground. Hope is important to keep while struggling against the current that tries to pull you out to sea. Hope will eventually get you to where your heart desires.

Sometimes, you realize that you have been going in the wrong direction and it can take four or five years to swim against the current, back to your right path. After redirecting yourself, you can travel the right course for several years before you see concrete manifestations. Hope keeps you oriented even when physical evidence is lacking. Eventually, the external environment will align to the movement of your inner truthful way. You may not know when the alignment will happen, so hope and patience allow you to endure the journey.

Perhaps what you are doing now feels meaningless. Try to give some energy to something that you believe in. Consistent effort will eventually reveal a substantial change. You will get a few moments of fulfillment along the way. You'll be less worn or weighed down with the meaningless when you make substantial steps toward your true beliefs. You do not have to leave the meaningless entirely or immediately—perhaps it pays the rent. But you can give yourself the gift of investment in the activity that feels meaningful.

So while we exist in *everything* (our interpretations and illusions), we can shift the concentration of our everything to a greater focus on internalizing reality and truths. These truths will never contradict each other, so your flow goes smoothly. A smooth flow is an attribute of peace.

Answers:

Without questions, there are no answers. So the beginning of finding answers is to question and yearn for more. Answers can come in the form of greater understanding, a shift in awareness and perspective, or improved relationships—all these bring you toward the flow of peace. The course of shifting concentration from interpreting truth to knowing truth is yearning (questioning) and opening your heart for answers.

We have two minds: the thinking mind and the heart mind. The thinking mind interprets and creates new ideas. The heart mind expressed our core yearning and connects to the harmony of the universe. The heart mind holds the wisdom of universal truth. The thinking mind can manifest the contents of the heart mind into concrete physical existence or it can create something else as reality. The heart mind is always aligned with the higher mind. (The higher mind is the core wisdom of all life.)

The heart's mind connects to both the basic life protecting instincts and the higher mind. We are not always aware of the thinking mind's creativity and the power that we give to it. The thinking mind's creativity does not make only good things, but also creates counterproductive ideas, which bring sorrow. For example, it can visualize efforts succeeding or failing. The creative mind limits and harms our efforts if it is disconnected from the higher mind. The heart mind longs for higher and higher being. It is the earth-heaven connection of physical principles and unseen unlimited spiritual principles together. We want to keep ourselves inside the boundaries that protect the good but also allow for creativity. The higher mind is both within the boundaries of good and is more creative than we currently are. Therefore the heart's longing is the magnet that drives us toward the higher mind so that we can become higher and higher in our own beings. When we shut down the heart's desire and focus on the grounded, practical brain or the creative, thinking mind, we experience a loss of control. We function best when these three are in balance: basic life sustaining practicality, creativity, and the heart's longing. Only then can we experience peace.

Listen *into* your heart to hear your longing. What questions does your heart long to answer?

Toughness:

Toughness and resilience can also be called perseverance. It is staying the course. The search for your true self can be more attractive than actually staying the course. In the search, there are many actual possibilities and a lot of fantasies that seem like possibilities. In staying the course, you know the way. You simply need to walk the way.

Dreaming is important because in our dreams we set goals. Then, as per usual, life happens and we have to get through obstacles. When we try our best and still get into impossible situations, we seek help through others. Energy is not created or destroyed. We just are. We are moving in directions. When you choose a direction, keep going there, even if you get pushed to the side or barriers are put in your way. Keep going deeper into your true heart's desire and go higher in your love and gratitude.

S.W.E.A.T.:

Stillness, work, everything, answers, and toughness: the walk for peace takes S.W.E.A.T. The activity of constant movement, change and growth is the course.

DREAM

REST

Remain –
You have no place to go

Ease –
Softness of flow
Breathe
For it is life
To breathe

Stop –
Energy cycling a doom
It is not even real
Do not you know that all things are growing?

Time –
Is better thought of as
Growth process
Maturing into good
You know
When growth is complete
Pluck the fruit, eat and
Rest

What is dreaming? Share your answer here:

The word *dream* can represent many ideas, from the ideal values and goals we carry throughout our lives to mental images occurring during sleep. The common thread between all the meanings is that dreams are non-material and potential. Dreaming can mean an inability to take action toward manifesting ideas or it can mean accessing hope. In *Peace*, I address dreams in both meanings: accessing hope and images that come in quiet, restful states.

Dreaming as accessing hope:

The heart's desire is our hope. Even in activity, a quiet state of mindfulness gives access to our heart's desire—our hope. "… desire fulfilled is the tree of life" Proverbs 13:12). Hope is a longing for a heart's desire and taking steps to fulfilling that desire. Feeling the absence of the heart's desire is as much a part of hope as its fulfillment. When a person lacks the tolerance to endure the feeling of absence, he or she may stop taking steps toward that desire. When no steps are taken to the heart's desire, hope is lost. Often, the person avoids hearing the heart's desire, because his or her choice of action (or inaction) fails to support hope. Then "Hope deferred makes the heart sick,…" Proverbs 13:12. A "sick heart" is a depressed, emotional, mental, and, soon after, a physical state of illness. Failing to take steps toward fulfilling dreams can eventually shut down a person's ability to dream. This person will most likely keep himself active, in order to avoid the quiet state where the heart's desire is revealed.

Dreaming as image in the quiet state:

Our minds and bodies are naturally programmed to go into quiet states. We can force the mind and body to stay active, but they will eventually go into hibernation and quiet down. Drugs can prevent the natural process and still nature eventually wins. The mind and body go into a quiet state called sleep. Whether we are mindful or not, we experiences our inner truth (dreams) during sleep.

A lot can be learned from dreams. If you want to remember your dreams, keep something within reach when you sleep that you can grab to record your dreams. You can have a pad and pen or an iPad, or a smartphone. Write out your dreams as they arise. In actuality, you are allowing your subconscious to express itself, so if new thoughts come up that you didn't necessarily have in the dream, record those, too. The thoughts are your deeper self speaking.

You can become your own mentor when you learn from your dreams. (Being your own mentor does not mean that you do not still need other people.) <u>The deeper wisdom within reveals itself to the quiet, resting self.</u>

Write a dream that you remember:

In a quiet restful state continue the dream and/or insights that you perceive from the dream:

Now that you are bringing your subconscious awareness into consciousness, continue the unfolding of dreams into goals. Follow your dream to identify your heart's desire and write some goals here:

The following is one of my dreams:

I was vertically lining sticks like matchsticks without sulphur tips. The sticks were a soft light wood and perfectly shaped with rounded square edges. The sticks were seven feet tall and four inches in diameter. Each stick lined up both front to back and across perfectly with even spaces between them. Even though this was a difficult obsessive-compulsive, perfectionist task, I only knew success. I had already lined up a large bunch and continued to line them up. These clean, flawless, light-yellow, natural, wood pillars were coming from within me. They represented the respect of individuals. The pure, natural pillars were, are, and will be pure individuals that are milled through relationships with me. I am reverent of each one and carefully place each stick prayerfully, respecting the uniqueness of each individual. The individual uniqueness is inherent in the unseen nature of the wood stick. All I see is the flawlessness. I see the pure core of the individuals and place them perfectly in the collective. I respect their uniqueness and do not focus on anything but the pure core of these people.

Just prior to the stacking part of the dream, I was with a new family of children—it was irrelevant whether they were blood-related. It was a new family. I am the mother, the support, and the nurturer. We had all gone to the bathroom and were regathering afterward. It felt a little chaotic and stressful as I couldn't access the boys in their bathroom. I had to depend on the father (my partner) to care for them while I devoted my energy to keeping track of the girls and pulling us all back together as a family. I had an envelope of tickets in my hand. I felt the urge to get upset and feel burdened. I caught myself, however, and chose joy and gratitude instead. I didn't feel it immediately, yet I set myself in the direction of joy—as opposed to stress. Finally, we were in line for a gentle roller coaster ride at an amusement park. One daughter—the overweight, dark-skinned teenager—didn't want to go on the ride. I preferred that we all went, yet I evaluated her needs and decided to wait with her at the little picnic tables while the rest of the family—the father and the other children—took the ride. There was a natural deep trust between the father and me, so my choice to stay back with the daughter was a choice that I could make on my own. He would trust that it was right. He would continue with the other children and we would all catch up again after the ride. I bought a smoothie for the daughter and gave her my personal time and attention. The other children were enjoying being together in a big group. The daughter with me was feeling insecure with the challenge of riding a scary roller coaster that the other family members were taking. I stayed with her this time. I felt that another time the father would stay with her and allow me to go with the big group. Also the big group would absorb us when they turned to less challenging or frightening activities. Each individual is respected and accepted and eventually lines up with perfect bright clean and flawless cores.

In another part of the dream, a tick is picked off one of the children by a wild bird. The tick is "yucky" and the children ask why such a bad thing needs to exist. I point out how the bird takes it as a treasure. It is good food for her chicks. The bird took it from where it didn't belong to where it would be treasured. Everything has its place. When it is in the wrong place it is yucky and disgusting. When in the right place, it is a treasure.

From this dream I can identify these goals: first, I want to be a "mill" for others to form into the perfect true beings; and second, I want a family with a deep trust in my partnership and a respect for the children's individual ability to manifest their true selves; and third, I want to put things in their proper place.

Dreams are one way that the subconscious accesses the conscious. You can develop the mindfulness to access deeper insight through other ways, too.

The following is an experience that came in a wakeful moment as insight to personal interactions. I woke up in the night and wrote the image with the same feeling as if I were dreaming. The insight came in a conscious form:

Waking Experience on June 11, 2011:

I feel shame—shame that I have needs, wants, and desires. (My subconscious thoughts are contradicting my reality.) The shame turns into anger against myself. (This is my maladaptive way of coping with my emotions.) Then I want to be rescued from my own feelings. In my desire to be rescued, I can turn my anger outward to a potential rescuer. When my rescuer is not managing my feelings, I feel rejected. Then the shame deepens—I am too much. I am too much to manage and too much to handle, so I have to be left, abandoned and rejected. There is no boundary drawn between my responsibility and the one who loves me. The one who loves me rejects me because I am too much. He or she can not continue simply to love me. He or she can not cope with my feelings or emotions. So he or she separates from me and lives as though I do not exist.

I am afraid to go there—to express what I am feeling and experiencing because I do not want to be too much. I do not want to be rejected.

The concepts of being too much and being rejected are ideas that I choose to use to explain a confused state of uncomfortable emotion. I do not need to choose those concepts. I could choose to stay in awareness of my unfulfilled desires—feeling the discomfort. Yet, when I can not tolerate the uncomfortable feelings I create exaggerated interpretations of the situation. I may have had a parent who cycled in idealizing and rejecting me, thus supporting me to form this concept. Wherever the concept originates does not matter.

What matters is if I want to continue this interpretation of myself or remain in a raw, truthful state that connects to my true identity.

Real relationship experiences make concrete changes to our thinking. For example, my early experiences created my concept of self as expressed above (being "too much" to love and being rejected). Fortunately, I have had other relationship experiences through therapists, pastors, and friends. I have some friends who have been very special to me because they have not rejected me, even when I felt at my worst. When I have been too much, they have set boundaries. My true friends do not withdraw their love, even when they have to withdraw their presence. The unavailability could feel like rejection, but I understand that they have their own need for self-care and need for protection from feeling overwhelmed. These balanced relationships help me reform my concept of self and support my connection to my truth.

Sometimes, relationships become strained when we use maladaptive coping skills. In those moments of disconnect, we want to stop talking and simply be taken care of. I want the world to bend around me. I start to reason that I bend around others so often that I need a turn. This is when my wants, needs, selfishness, shame, and fear of rejection cycles. I tend to retreat—to turn on myself, stifle myself. This becomes anger toward myself, which is depression. The only way out of the cycle is to recognize that I am not 100 percent responsible for who I am—my feelings, my desires, etc. God created me with my basic character, wants, needs, desires, and emotions. I can enhance or distort those with my choices. I can use maladaptive coping mechanism to distort myself into my own enemy—like I do in the cycle. Or I can recognize who I am—my wants, needs, and feelings and be grateful for them. I can be grateful to God for them and for the breath that carries me like the ocean that I can float on when I relax and trust it. Then I can put my focus on the Source of life—the Source of love, the Source of my dreams, desires, needs and feelings. I can give gratitude and glory to the Source of life. Then I give gratitude and glory to my true self, because the Source of life is the source of the essence of my true being. Yet, I do not focus on me. I focus on the Source of love—like turning my face to the sun and appreciating the sun. In doing so I am bathed in sunlight, warmth, and life's energy. And I do not have to do anything to receive abundance. All I have to do is turn my face to the sun and stay still, appreciating.

I want to sunbathe like this with others, too. Sometimes my friends and I get caught in a fear-shame cycle. Someone needs to turn his or her head to the sun. Then others will then be reminded to turn to appreciate the Source with gratitude and glory. I love sunbathing in Supreme Love. How do I translate this to a physical-world experience? I believe that it's a collective, "How do we create the community environment?" question.

Include your answer here:

My attempt to answer follows:

As I strengthen my awareness of the Source of love—living and expressing through my own being—I can become more aware of this force in others. I can see the love and discern the other energies from it. As I relate to the love energy, feed it, and starve the other energies, I direct my life into the gratitude that creates peace. At the same time, the other person's life moves into gratitude toward peace or they depart from me. Since people have a need to relate, if enough people feed the love energy and starve the other energies, we will need to engage in love energies in order to relate to other people. Living with a personal focus on feeding love energies will become a collective gratitude or peace.

The Source of the Heartbeat

Consoles
Within your little heart

In the consoling you release the pain—
From lost opportunities
From misunderstanding parents
From an absent spouse

Consoling
And releasing pain
'Til
Your heart glows
In pure white light

A heartbeat
Tolerates
Consoling
The pain of others

Turning the darkness
Into life

Those people
Who touch hearts
With the pure light
Of consolation
Received from
The Source
Move souls

They are the Ones Remembered

Great successes are made with pixels of positive effort

BEAUTY

Peace in self—core spirit

Peace in body—core abdomen—
Holds body structurally.
The place where breath is created physically,
The "mind" of the body.

Center of mind flows through Chakras.
The heart chakra is the center of all seven Chakras
Connecting physical earth and spiritual heaven.

The emotional center is the lower heart and abdomen.
As emotions climb to joy they rest in the heart.
As they descend into fear, the dwell in the abdomen.

Focusing being into the heart and breath
Creates peace in the individual.

Peace among two people
Begins with peace in the individuals.

A person
Only has control
Over maintaining his or her own
Individual peace—
Yet it can be infectious—

Inspiring others' peace.

Beauty

Beauty, like love, is a choice of action. We show beauty outwardly to create a world of beauty. Yet the inner world may look messy. Take the body, for example: we groom and dress the outer self. Yet, the part of the body under the skin is an unattractive sight of blood and guts. A perfect figure skating routine looks beautiful and full of ease, yet behind the scenes are many bruises, falls, frustrations, fears, and disappointments. The public presentation is the refined beauty. I have friends that always look beautiful and make others feel good. They have many complications and traumas in their lives, but they present the beauty. We always have a choice of what energy we put into the world. Sharing beauty will reflect beauty back.

Sometimes we feel the need to put "out there" what is inside of us regardless of its ugliness. I believe this need is to verify the truth of our experience. In my first book, *Being,* my emphasis was about accepting our experiences as being real. I know from my own life that when we feel we're being talked into disregarding our own experiences and accepting someone else's interpretation, we can feel frustrated, crazy, and nullified. I believe that when we feel our experiential reality being challenged, we need to get it "out there" to have it verified by another person. Often we do not know how to express that reality and we embellish it with assumptions and ideas.

Take the example of an imaginary conversation between a ten-year-old girl and her mother to illustrate the subtlety of adult embellishments.

The daughter tells her mother with anger and frustration, "My teacher is stupid." The child is experiencing something unpleasant from the teacher. The mother responds, "Your teacher is not stupid. She'd never have graduated college and become a teacher if she were stupid." The mother negates her daughter's experience in her attempt to help the girl express her true experience.

"She really is stupid. I won't talk to her," replied the girl.

"You are upset with her. What makes you upset with her?" (The mother verifies the girl's real experience by identifying her emotion. Then she helps her daughter identify the cause of her feelings.)

The girl continues, "She said that people who pray to solve their problems do not solve problems."

"You felt your teacher was criticizing mom and dad. That makes you angry." (The mother verifies the cause of her feelings.)

"She said they didn't make anything better. She's so stupid."

"And you know from your experience that praying has solved problems and you have seen us pray to make a lot of things better." (The mother verifies the girl's experience.)

"Yes. She's a liar and she's stupid. She shouldn't be a teacher. She teaches lies." (This is true from the girl's experience. This is her truthful and verifiable reality.)

The mother explains, "Even teachers do not know everything. Your teacher knows what she has experienced. Most likely she does not use prayer to solve problems, so she assumes that prayer does not solve problems. You, on the other hand, have used prayer to help you solve problems and you have an experience. She can only teach from her experience and she can not teach what she does not know herself. But she can teach what she does know like reading and writing and math." (The mother helps the girl discern qualities and look at the big picture with clarity. The mother teaches her daughter not to make an assumption about a person based on a few facts.)

"I bet she's a witch."

"You're very angry with her. Even though you are angry, it's not right to make up and say something about another person that may not be true, especially if it's hurtful. I understand that she hurt your feelings by telling the class something you felt was wrong from your personal experience. Do you want to create more hurt? Do you want to copy your teacher's hurtful action, so you can become like her in this aspect?" (The mother helps her daughter distinguish between reality—her real experience—and her imagination—driven by an emotion)

In creating peaceful action, the hardest thing to do may seem simple and insignificant. The thing to do is to not retaliate. Loving is a simple effort that is made difficult when the winds of emotion, self-righteousness, and indignation interfere. Even the person who is completely loving experiences those winds. When those who succumb to retaliation see the person who is entirely loving, they cannot bear to believe that there is a person who fails to succumb to retaliation. Then they create difficulties for him or her by giving him or her cause to feel greater indignation. This is called persecution—unjust accusation and harm.

In order to remove the emotional trigger responses, you need to have discipline. Choose to express beautiful, not ugly actions. A person can always do with his or her emotions as he or she chooses. Emotions are real. Listen to them. Then with the higher mind, choose an action that fits your goal. If peace is the goal—choose the actions that move us toward Peace. I say "us", specifically, because I have found that there is no complete and enduring individual peace without collective peace.

A world of peace does not mean a world without conflict. Conflict is the stimulus for growth. Growth is the verb of life. Breathing, being, and growing are key elements of life. Conflict is the pushing of one entity against the other—like one idea or tradition against another. The sprout creates conflict with the soil surrounding the seed and presses against the soil toward sunlight. Conflict is simply the push—not the resolution of the conflicting entities.

Think of some conflicts that you have had (or are having) and imagine expressing beauty, truth, and love together to move through the conflict. Simply write down several different ways of resolving the conflict, then circle the one that most expresses beauty, truth, and love.

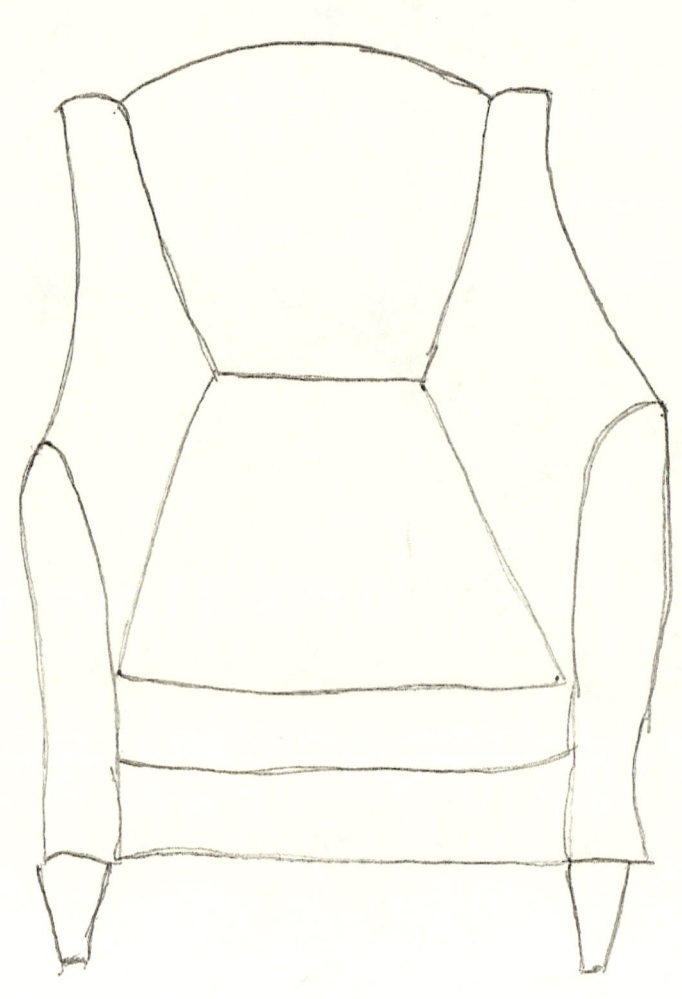

TRUTH

Watch your thoughts;
they become words.

Watch your words;
they become actions.

Watch your actions;
they become habits.

Watch your habits;
they become character.

Watch your character;
it becomes your destiny.

Lao-Tzu.

Truth

The question of "finding" one's true self may be the result of a semantic confusion. I see the issue of finding oneself more accurately expressed as co-creating yourself into the person with whom you are pleased and who harmonizes with truth in the universe. Ultimately this means to be in harmony with the universal principle and a reflection of the original Creator.

The process of co-creating the self is both fully in your control and directed by universal principles. Choices have natural consequences. The consequences are what many people call karma. Pain tolerance is what allows us to persist in creating bad karma. The statement, "blessed are the poor in spirit," expresses how strength to endure pain and misery only prolongs the change that is necessary to realign with truth. Actions that violate universal principles get answered with universal principles.

The following is an exercise in finding Peace through being truthful.

Redirect your thoughts and remain truthful:

Your experience is real. What you sense, feel, and receive from your environment is your truth. However, we quickly take this raw experience and translate it into thought. Raw physical senses (sight, hearing, touch, taste, and smell) combine with raw emotion (fear, joy, anger, sadness, confusion). Most often, the raw experience is instantaneously churned in the thinking machine and woven into a thought. So, for example, seeing your best friend walk down the hall with someone else and not notice you, combined with a fear sensation becomes the thought, *I feel rejected*. The raw experience moved quickly into what we call a feeling, although it is actually a thought. If we slow down the process, we catch it from raw experience to thought: *She's not with me. She's with someone else. She does not like me anymore. She's mad at me.* There are a myriad of memories, interpretations of other experiences, and thoughts that are part of the process, which occurs instantaneously, moving you away from your raw experience—moving you away from truth.

Since thoughts become actions and ultimately become your life destiny, you change your life and destiny by redirecting your thoughts. The following is a process for redirecting thoughts:

1) First, identify your thoughts. Many "feelings" are actually thoughts. They are not the raw experiences.
2) Identify the raw experiences (your raw emotions and senses). Meditation or mindfulness is the practice that brings a person back to raw experience.
3) Rephrase your raw experience into a thought that directs you to a hopeful outcome.
4) Realize that everything is an opportunity and you make the choices in your opportunities

Take the above example of the friend you see with someone else. We identified the thought, *I feel rejected*. We rewind the thought back to the raw experience—*I see my friend, I feel fear*. Make a choice to replace fear with love. You could churn out this thought, *My friend looks happy and that makes me smile. I'll ask her to schedule lunch with me*. This redirection moves toward receiving joy through a love connection and building greater joy in the relationship. Without the stimulus of seeing your friend with someone else, you may not have thought to ask your friend to lunch. The experience created an opportunity. There are many choices to redirect the same situation. Whatever choice you make is your own, as are the consequences. If you are unhappy with your life, redirect your thoughts. Own them—do not let them own you.

Okay, now do you understand this concept? Well, you can not truly know it until you live it. Here comes the work. Practice the redirection. You may feel as clumsy as a two-year old trying to tie shoelaces. But remember that you were once that clumsy two-year old and you can now tie shoes without even having to think. (If you followed the last two statements, you just practiced a redirection of thought). All you have to do is make a choice to practice redirection. Then you will be heading into a new direction in your own life.

The simple first step is to breathe and become aware of your experience. Feel your body. Notice your breath. Notice the sounds and the sensations on your skin. Observe your environment. If any thoughts arise, catch them, and redirect them.

To where are you redirecting them? Go back to the dream chapter to see your goals; work with them. Goals that follow your deep heart's desire will create your happiness and become your peace.

Redirection Exercise:
Breathe. Then write your truths to these points.

Day 1:
Sensations in my body:

I hear:

I feel on my skin:

I see:

Emotional feeling:

Thought:

Redirected thought:

Repeat this exercise often. Practice once a day for seven days (six more copies of the exercise below). Continue if you like and/or repeat the exercise more often during the day. You can keep a separate journal for this exercise. Remember, this is for yourself. It is not homework for any teacher or authority. Use the exercise however you like—there's no wrong way to do it.

Day 2:
Sensations in my body:

I hear:

I feel on my skin:

I see:

Emotional feeling:

Thought:

Redirected thought:

Day 3:
Sensations in my body:

I hear:

I feel on my skin:

I see:

Emotional feeling:

Thought:

Redirected thought:

Day 4:
Sensations in my body:

I hear:

I feel on my skin:

I see:

Emotional feeling:

Thought:

Redirected thought:

Day 5:
Sensations in my body:

I hear:

I feel on my skin:

I see:

Emotional feeling:

Thought:

Redirected thought:

Day 6:
Sensations in my body:

I hear:

I feel on my skin:

I see:

Emotional feeling:

Thought:

Redirected thought:

Day 7:
Sensations in my body:

I hear:

I feel on my skin:

I see:

Emotional feeling:

Thought:

Redirected thought:

The Invisible

The invisible elements are the most important: love, faith, vision, trust, passion, hope, and breath.

The visible elements are a testament to the invisible. You may wear nice clothes. The clothes were merely fibers, like dust, until vision, hope, love, faith, and breath transformed those dust fibers into the handsome garment that you wear. Any "thing" that you have or own came from the invisible.

What about peace? What are the visible and invisible elements of peace?

Explore with me. I'll start and you add to the list:

Invisible elements:

- Love
- Hope
- Faith
- Respect
- Compassion

Visible:

- Smiling lively people
- Intact families
- Beautiful neighborhoods
- Health—no gunshot wounds
- Fewer trauma patients in the hospital—more eldercare
- Acts of kindness
- Absence of physical, verbal, emotional violence
- Many cultures respecting one another

Truth and Belonging

The ability to enhance our experience with another person's perspective is the mechanism that allows change for growth. In a healthy sense, it expands our reality toward greater maturation. For example, an infant's view of the front of a teddy bear is expanded to recognize the back as well, when he accepts the mother's perspective of the bear as she sits across from the child holding the teddy bear. Another example is the hungry child who will stop screaming when he expands his experience to the mother's, who needs time to prepare the food for the child. We continue throughout our lives to expand our experience by allowing other's experiences to move in with our direct experiences.

Problems arise when the other person's experience contradicts or negates our own. When your own experience is rejected for the sake of relating to another person, then you damage yourself. An example is when you have seen something and another person says, ""You couldn't have seen that." Perhaps you saw an expression of anger (or sadness) on their face and the person cannot accept their own experience of anger (or sadness). Then the person who cannot accept his or her emotional experience invests great effort into placing his or her own false and distorted perspective into you in order to push out your genuinely perceived reality. He or she withholds the relationship from you until you accept the false and distorted perspective into your experience of reality.

The problem is that what you accept for the sake of keeping the relationship is not reality, but an altered reality. An altered reality will always battle with genuine reality. A mind that holds altered realities will always be in conflict with the original, genuine mind within. This leads to a conflicted person. Like a body with a virus, the mind will be ill and carry symptoms of battling the foreign object to return to original health. In the body, those symptoms can be a rash, sneezing, or a fever, etc. In the mind, those symptoms can be confusion, self-punishing thoughts, or depression, for example. A healthy mind lives in love, hope, and resonance with natural truth. The practice of mindfulness is investing energy into the awareness of love, hope, and truth. We need mindfulness to wash away the elements of distortion that we acquire in our relationships with others who reject our genuine experiences and replace them with distortions. Perhaps we have practiced reinterpreting our genuine experiences into a reality that allowed us to connect with others. We do this in order to feel belonging.

Belonging allows us to succumb to peer pressure and other cultural pressures. At one time in history the acceptable perspective was to believe that the world was flat. Those who believed otherwise experienced rejection and loneliness. Only after some brave people risked their lives to follow their own inner truth, to live with a new belief and wander beyond the perceived boundary, did other people's perspectives change. Imagine being on one of Columbus's ships heading toward the horizon, while knowing that the common belief is that there's an end off of which the ship will fall. Where the ship would fall, you wouldn't know. It would be some sort of end, an unknown, scary death. The false and distorted belief of a limited perception of reality is unable to continue as truthfulness presses forth. For Columbus and his crew, their genuine perception viewed the horizon moving as they moved toward it. Distorted beliefs are replaced by genuine truths with life lessons and experience. As more people have similar experiences, perceptions of truth are shared.

Peace—No Peace

People with similar experiences
Feel belonging
To each other.

If you invest in
The people
who want to mature
into greater love, truth and hope,
you will
belong
in greater love, truth and hope.
I hope to travel with you.

If you give
Energy to a person
who does
Not want to expand their perception,
who wants to keep his or her "reality",
You invest in inertia.
No movement occurs.
There's no reward.
The investment of energy results in frustration,
like pushing an unmovable stone.

Free will prevails.

Save your energy
from the Push.

While people may disagree on what truth is, there is a universal truth. Individual truth is real and pertains to an individual. Yet, universal principles affect all individuals. Universal principles cannot be squeezed into a single perspective like a group of laws or methods. The purpose of the laws and methods are to guide us into knowing the principles of life. Knowing comes from our own seeking, our experiences, and our efforts to absorb understanding.

Think of some basic common truths and make your list here:

For example:
Being forbidden to have your own experience is psychological torture. When a reinterpretation of your perception pushes out your reality and gives your genuine awareness no space to exist, you might feel crazy.

LOVE

Love

L-O-V-E is a word that attempts to express the greatest power ever. Even defining the entity as "power" does not give it justice. Calling it an "entity" is beneath the full expression of the meaning of love. Love is a verb and a noun. Love is perhaps the source of life. Yet, look at the many expressions of "love". There is the mother who makes her dinner of the scraps of left-over foods from her children's plates, not ever letting them know that she sacrifices her meals for them. There is the child who hears, "I love you" while he feels the pain from bruises imparted by the "loving" parent. There is the father who fights his sleep deprivation, hiding his concern that his company is not bringing in a profit, so that he can work harder and allow his family to feel secure. There are the butterflies in the heart when a young woman is adored by a young man. There is the desire to make a card for Grandma because, "I am happy she is coming to read me stories again!" For all these (and more) expressions we give the same name of love.

I see words as the boxcars on a train of a sentence that carry meaning. The name of the boxcar may say "Fresh Milk" yet the contents are poison chemicals. The content is what gets delivered regardless of the name of the outside of the car. A person may say, "I love you," after verbally abusing you. Another person may seem harsh by saying, "I do not want you here with me." But beneath the words is a deep love that pushes the other toward fulfilling his or her own dreams (instead of caretaking a loved one). True love is always directed toward making possibilities for the best outcome for the person.

It is often said that, "Behind every successful man is a great woman." I have seen that successful men have had great women in their lives—wives, mothers, sisters, and friends. Perhaps, for a man, the women in his life provide the foundation from which he steps forth. I say, "Behind every beautiful woman, is a man who loves her (and makes her glow)."

The first woman and first man in our lives affect us profoundly.

Mothers seem to be the foundation of any person's life. At a bare minimum, a person spends the first nine months of formation in very close relation to the mother. Her thoughts, words, and actions embrace the forming child. Fathers help form the identity of a child through his interaction with him or her. A girl's self-esteem is correlated to how her father relates to her. Simple observation reveals that children pick up attitudes and behaviors from the people around them. (Adults do the same, yet children are exponentially impacted). A parent's relationship with the child is the child's foundation of love.

In adult life, the women with whom a man surrounds himself, in his intimate milieu, affect who he is. The feminine space sets a direction through the shape of her area of allowance and her boundaries. Also, for women—the women she surrounds herself with set a direction and affect who she is. (Here, the use of intimate space is not equated with sexual contact - that may be included. I use intimate space or intimate milieu to mean when we allow a person to engage us in their emotions, beliefs, and thought processes in a way that touches the soul.) Women tend to engage in intimate space more readily than men. Yet, when men enter the intimate milieu of a relationship they affect their love object strongly and can alter who that person becomes. A visual metaphor I have is of a rocket (masculine energy) on a launch pad (feminine space). The launch pad is the foundation from which the rocket propels itself. The launch pad gives the direction to the projectile. The concept of feminine space explains why many men can perform the same job with different outcomes. For example, many men have lead nations to prosperity or destruction. Many men have built things with varying grades of quality, usefulness and attraction. Many men give speeches with greater or lesser success in motivating the listeners. The things that a man produces are expressions of the man and come to identify the man. The foundation of perspectives, meaningfulness, and direction that he has is reflected in his product. This is all true for women, too. As human beings, we are made of both masculine and feminine energy. A man feels his masculinity strongest when in the presence of full feminine energy. A woman experiences herself as a woman strongest in receiving masculine energy. The experience is as good as the love is pure and true. This concept pertains to all types of relationships, not just love relationships. (My next book, *Full: About Food, Sex, and Creativity*, will include greater explanation of masculine-feminine interaction and power.)

The theme of love as a peace element speaks to who or what is allowed in your intimate space, because the elements in the intimate space direct your actions. Your actions determine who you become—a peacemaker or something else. I have seen people march forward speaking of peace while leaving a trail of broken people and broken relationships behind them.

You call
Tired, defeated, hopeless,
Giving up.
I wonder...

Who was in your intimate space?

Peace in Death

I chose to love.
Therefore I chose to hurt.
As all things in life change,
the thing I have
becomes the thing I lost
and the thing I lost
becomes the thing I have.

I have a daughter who had a little dog.
My daughter went to school.
I got her dog.
The dog was killed.
I lost my companion.
I have an added aspect of love with my daughter.

A Dog named Kat

She lived one year and eleven days—a short yet significant life. She didn't stay with us on earth into the year of the Water Dragon.

Kat, a six-pound twelve-ounce Malteese-Yorky (Morky) was a little, soft, warm, and delicate, living bundle of love. I cry when I say "was." Does not love live forever? Is not love before beginnings and beyond endings? Is not love just an eternal "I am"?

The life has left her body. Where is the life soul now?

I just want to reach for those I love and embrace them.

I encourage you to write about your experiences with love that has endured beyond death:

I share one of my experiences here:

My daughter had wanted a hand-held pet that she could bring with her everywhere. I took my daughter to the miniature dog shop. We fell in love with the little Morky that my daughter named Katherine Ann, "Kat."

Kat lived in our arms and laps. She became an extra appendage to my daughter, as her mother, and me, as her grandmother. When my daughter was at school, Kat stayed with me. My life changed. My life shifted to make space for Kat. I went to bed at nine thirty p.m. to fit her sleeping pattern. She slept with me on the bed and would get up from her curled slumber if I left the room. She would stay at my feet. (She was so small that I wouldn't see her under me.) When we woke, we would go straight to my bathroom first and then quickly I would put on her leash, collar, coat, and my own coat and boots before heading out the door so she could do her business in the yard. Every morning, we walked down the hill together to the post office to get my mail. Then we ate breakfast together before I took her in the car to the gym. She would stay in the car while I worked out. Then we would go for a walk down the empty road to a utility station. We met with friends for doggie play dates. Then Kat would sleep quiet on my lap or the sofa near me while I would write or work.

Kat was with me all the time. She came out on errands. She slept in my lap as I drove to see my daughter and shadowed my daughter after we arrived. Kat loved my daughter so much—always followed her and looked for her when she wasn't around. Kat was pure love—extreme love. I think she was the first love that my daughter completely let in to her being. I felt Kat and my daughter were bonded in souls. Kat bonded my daughter to the love of life. Kat's soul and love being is attached to my daughter. Perhaps Kat's love was so strong that she needed to be freed from the physical separation and now she can live with and in my daughter. That's the reality I would like to believe and experience. I would like my daughter to experience Kat's love in every hug, in every step and every breath of life.

We were blessed to have Kat in our lives for the past seven months. We were touched with a deep love through her little life.

She was also loved very deeply. We learned to love from our little six-pound, twelve-ounce soft teacher.

It hurts so much that she left this life. She died as she lived— quick and lively, with love and excitement. She was hit by a car and died suddenly—no pain, just fun and love until the tire crushed her body. Her last breath popped out of her and left her eyes still smiling. I carried her little body to the closest vet. He tried to revive her. She had died upon impact. There was no suffering. She didn't deserve suffering. True love is not about suffering. She was and is pure love. She is showing me that my love is not big enough and pure enough yet, because my heart is suffering, as I miss her. May I grow into the great love that Kat already is.

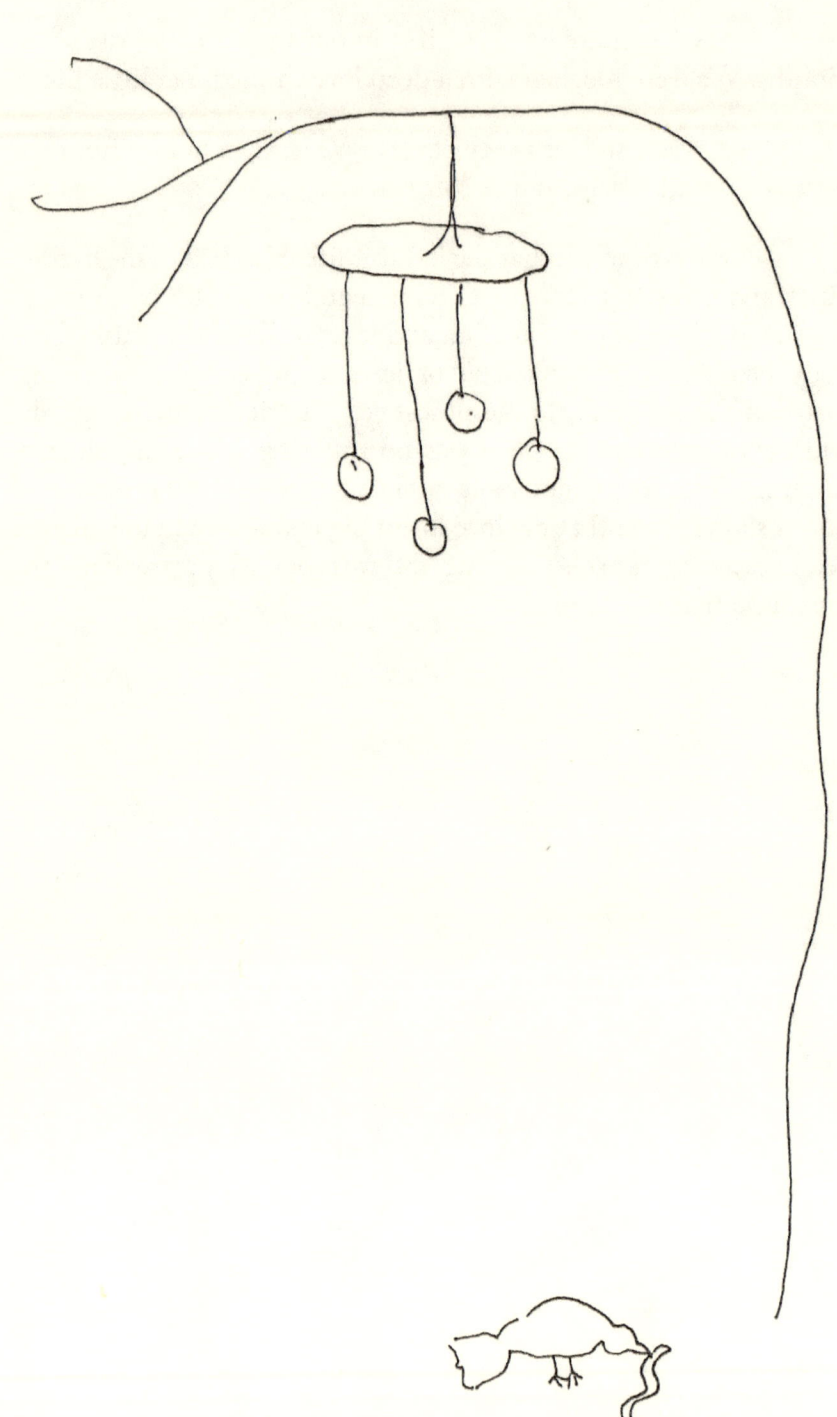

VALUE

Mon Dieu
Mon Dieu
Il veut
Elle veut
Tout le monde veut
Mais c'est n'est pas possible,
Touts les desirs

My God
My God
He wants
She wants
The whole world wants
But it's not possible
All the wants

We can never have peace
If we focus on wants.

Mon Dieu
Mon Dieu
Qu'est ce que Vous voulez?
Aimez
Aimez
Aimez
C'est n'est pas les choses
Ni les actes de bonté
C'est l'adoration de la vie
Qui donne de la Paix.

Oh God
Oh God
What do you want?
Love
Love
Love
It's not the things
Nor the good acts
It's the adoration of life
That brings Peace.

Value

Value speaks to our priorities. What do we spend our time and energy on? In my early twenties, I took a seminar on time management. The seminar was developed for achievement in business, although it pertained generally to success in life as well. One of the exercises I did for the seminar was writing down how I spent every moment of my day for several days. Then I went back and simply observed how I was spending my time. In the evaluation process, I could see that how I spent my time was very different than how I thought I was spending it. I could see that my actual priorities were very different than my perceived priorities. Seeing the contradiction directed me toward a more honest observation of my values. This included dropping my judgments about values and looking at how my actual priorities were serving me. I had to discover how some activities that I considered useless, were actually very useful. For example, I felt that sitting with a person in small talk was a waste of time in business. Yet, accumulatively, I spent a lot of time in simple conversations. As a young adult, I had failed to understand the value of listening and being with a person simply to acknowledge and enjoy their being. I had felt that we had to be producing something measurable in every moment. I would be frustrated with myself for "wasting time in trivialities." I came to understand that the small things are the important components of great things.

Great accomplishments are actually a collection of the pixels of positive acts.

Consistency is the route to manifestation. While I always liked to write down my thoughts, I wrote when I felt like it—inconsistently. I valued writing and wanted to become a writer who produced books to share my thoughts with others. I realized that if I wrote regularly until I finished a book, I would become a writer. After trying to take up water skiing on a vacation, I realized that I was no longer in the athletic shape that I used to be and my ability to ski was affected by my muscular weakness. I started a daily stretching routine and exercised vigorously three to five times a week to build strength and endurance. Even though I would probably water ski only one or two weeks each year, I knew that the consistency of effort would allow me to be in shape for the activity.

The following exercise will help you identify what you truly value:

Look at how you spend your day. Take some paper or a little notebook and record everything that you do for three days. Be as detailed as you can. After the three days look at where you spend your time. (Do not look at it during the three days of recording.) From where you spend your time, you will know what your actual priorities are. Use the next three blank pages of this book to record your insight.

What do value and consistency have to do with building a world of peace? When you are doing one thing, there are an infinite amount of other things you are not doing.

Many people think of peace as a passive thing—that when there is no fighting, there is peace. Any teacher, mother, caretaker, or leader can verify that if you do not have a positive activity to direct the child or follower in, destructive activity may set in. For example, if you give a young child crayons and paper without direction to use the crayons to draw on the paper, the child may break or eat the crayons and rip up the paper. The action is not bad; it just is not directed toward building something. If there is a group of children, one child may want to throw the crayon, another child wants to break the crayons, and another child may want to eat the crayons. They will start fighting because they want different things of the same crayons. None of the wants are bad they are just incompatible with each other. If there is no guide or leader to direct them on what to do with the crayons, they will fight until someone wins and others lose. A lot of hurt and damage may occur in that process. A good leader in this situation would listen to the wants of each child and determine a direction for the group. The leader or teacher may have his or her own idea of what to do with the crayons. If he or she validates each want, each child feels valued. Then, by giving value and respect to the children, the leader or teacher may receive enough respect from the children for them to comply with the teacher's direction.

COMPASSION

Hovering Compassionately

The sun is rising into the sky
over the calm waters and vegetation.
The birds are rallying their songs
from tree to tree in stereo.
I am present in the world;
aware of the stature of my body,
aware of the environment that I see and hear,
taking in the light without burning my skin.
God is so profoundly present
and I am dull in experiencing Him.
Separated—
I listen to gentle waves break on the sea
and think it's just noise.
Yet God
is whispering to me over and over
like a pre-language infant.
all I hear is noise.
I fail to extract the message from the sounds.
A variety of palm trees stand before me
with intricate strokes of beauty.
I observe this artwork
with ignorance,
simply noticing the green color,
and the fanning shape.
I fail to read the expression this artist conveys in His choice of
color, shape, and composition. And what an amazing piece of art
that allows each individual
to obtain his or her unique composition
depending upon the perspective of approach.

Like the swaddled infant,
I do not know what I am experiencing.
While sounds and sights are familiar,
I merely take them in without making sense of them.
Regardless,
the Parent holding me
continues to communicate to me—
a one-way conversation.
I may babble back
thinking that my sounds are meaningful.
My Parent is thrilled with the effort I make to respond
even though my sounds make no sense at all.
How long will He find my babbles satisfying?
At what point does His heart sink
realizing that this child is retarded –
slow to learn to communicate.
At what point does He cry
at the prolonged loneliness
of reaching out with no reply?
My Parent never gives up on me.
He continues to hold me
swaddled at his breast
speaking to me
hoping that at any moment
I will grasp the message
and utter a sensible reply.

Compassion Peace

Compassion is openness, respect and action. Openness allows for the presence of other. The recognition of other is an initial respect that is sustained with continuing respect. Allowing the experience of the other to come into my own experience helps me feel and become aware of the other's reality. Then with my comprehension of the other's reality, I can act to support higher quality of life in the other. The other could be an aspect within myself or another person or thing. When my actions are aligned with higher wisdom, they are compassionate actions of peace.

Compassion within

You can connect your consciousness to higher wisdom. In the moment of connection you have a flash of higher awareness that directs you to peace. After the flash of wisdom, your body could say, "I am hungry. I am tired. I want to move." How do you connect that higher wisdom to action in the physical body? Peace in the individual is the harmonious connection of the higher spirit to the body. Just like two people with different lifestyles have trouble getting along, a person's mind and body that has different lifestyles struggles to harmonize. If truth (the purpose of scripture) is God's food for the mind, what is God's food for the body? What is the method for connecting your consciousness of higher wisdom to actions in your body?

The body needs health in order to support health in the spirit. Scriptures give directions for proper care of the body in order to bring it into harmony with a higher spirit. Science provides many instructions for biological health, as well. The mind's lack of compassion for the body or the body's lack of compassion for the mind is the beginning of the disconnection and disharmony between the mind and body.

Compassion with Others

Opening ourselves to the experience of others with respect begins compassion. When we bind our lives by the rules of our belief systems, we can be closed to another person's experience. Individuals, groups, corporations and other entities abide by principals within their chosen philosophies. Some of those philosophies do not fit with one another. Compassion unlocks the hold that prevents us from seeing others in their reality. In creating a world of peace, we loosen the binds to belief systems and look for the harmonious principles of peace. We regard each other with open minds and respect. Peace principles directed with compaction lead us to peace actions with one another.

Listening and letting a person express him or herself is a major practice of maturing peace. Listening does not mean you agree with what the person says. It is just about letting another person express his or her true self. Through expressing self, a person gets the opportunity to see from the outside who they are in the inside. Their being is always changing. Seeing oneself through expression allows a person to choose a direction that would take them into a finer expression of self.

Compassion for others starts with compassion for yourself. You want to live as your true self. Many people question, "Who am I?" and set on a quest to "find myself." The question of "finding" one's true self may be a confusion of semantics. I see the issue of "finding" yourself more accurately expressed as developing into being with whom you are pleased. Ultimately, this means a being that is in harmony with universal principles and a reflection of the original Creator.

Since the beginning of compassion is being open to listen, listen to yourself. Ask yourself, "How would I look if I were my perfect self?" Now loosen the binds of belief systems and listen. Follow the exercise on the next page.

Complete the following thoughts:

My perfect self would react to a mistake by:

My perfect self would eat:

My perfect self would do these things every day:

My perfect self would treat my mother this way:

My perfect self would say this to my father:

My perfect self can see:

My perfect self would have these thoughts repeating in my mind:

My perfect self would spend free time:

My perfect self cares most about:

My perfect self wakes up with this thought:

My perfect self would do this to close the day:

Others would say this about my perfect self:

All of your answers to this exercise are thoughts that you can turn into actions. You have a choice. No one controls who you are, but you. Any choice you make is fine, as long as you do not blame your choice on anything else. Love and forgive yourself. Then make a new choice in each new moment. You may jot down some possible choices of action here.

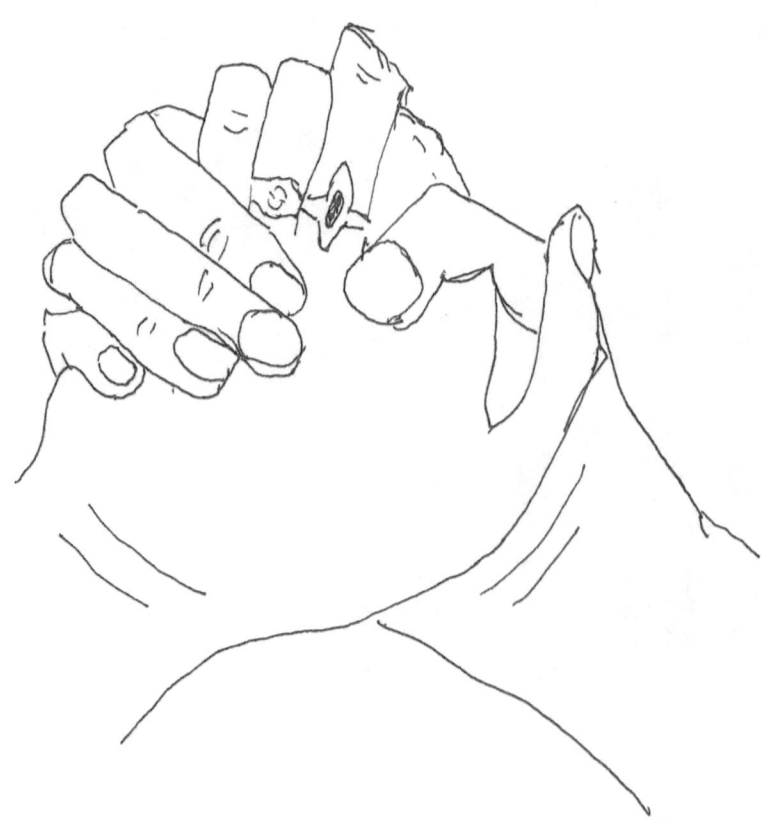

JUSTICE

Justice

In a dream
I experienced a scene of forgiveness
between a police woman and the woman caught breaking the law.
The dream
was like an expressionistic piece of art
in its ability to convey principle of relationships.
Use your mind's eye to create this picture:

A large tough woman
uniformed as a prison guard
stands before
a delicate, guilty woman
such as the woman who was going to be stoned in front of Jesus.
The two women clasp hands
Look down at their feet
with toenails painted bright red
their clasped hands
also have bright red fingernail polish
the two Women are asking for and giving forgiveness.

The forgiveness is a meal
That goes up through plastic tubing
To astronauts in space -
men exploring Infinity
being held safely by life cords of genuine love.

Opposite type women
joined in forgiveness bonds
create grounding roots
for men to explore Infinity.

Write your interpretation of this dream:

My interpretation (the truth I need to hear now):

We all have law enforcers (regulators) and rebels (explorers) in us. Each person must access the "policewoman" and "the biblical radical woman who breaks the rules" within. Those two aspects of self must bow in humility and clasp hands in forgiveness. The bright red nail polish is strong and draws attention stating that this internal forgiveness is extremely important. Each person who grounds in inner forgiveness will be able to explore infinity. The inner forgiveness and reconciliation will translate into outer creativity, including building good relationships.

We are creators—
Co-creators with the original Creator.
Quantum physicists have a theory that our scientific "explorations"
to discover the universe may be more projection of our
thoughts than finding things that are already out there.

Possibly,
humans are creating the universe
through thoughts.

Mindfully,
we can control
which thoughts to feed and which ones to starve.

The thoughts we feed,
we will manifest.

Fear thoughts
will manifest our fears;
thoughts that focus on our hopes
will produce our heart's desire.

Therefore,
I make my effort to fast from fears—
have no fears.

May each person fast from fears.
Let's put all our energies into feeding hopes and dreams.

Justice naturally prevails at the time a lesson is learned. I read a statement once: "There are no mistakes except the ones you do not learn from." A person with the strategy to benefit from other person's mistakes believes he is a winner, yet in reality is the loser. He maneuvers around the opportunity to learn lessons for growth as he presses toward his narcissistic illusion—the illusion of "I am a winner because I made the other person lose." This is a person without a meaningful goal. The person with a goal may be victim to the "I win, you lose" strategist, yet in pressing toward the meaningful goal, he becomes an even greater winner.

Higher wisdom, which is reflected in many different scriptures, explains this concept of justice in different ways. Jesus said, "But seek first the kingdom of God and his righteousness, and all these things will be added to you." (Mathew 6:33). In Buddhism, the expression is to believe in the universe's vow to give you happiness, and then all doubts disintegrate.

Having a meaningful goal is the beginning of justice. Return to the chapter titled "Dream" to engage and develop your meaningful goal. Your meaningful goal is your big goal—the mark you leave in history and the sum of your life. Focusing on the meaningful goal allows for all the problems to resolve as you lead your life purposefully, instead of reacting to what it presents you. Justice occurs when the problems become secondary to the effort toward the goal.

If you have a personal experience of focusing on your goal first and your problems seeming to solve themselves as you focus, write that experience here. (It will help you remember the next time you get overwhelmed by problems):

Dilemma

Three conflicting elements:

1) Each person
has an equal value and potential for goodness.

2) Some people
create negative energy and are destructive to others.

3) Each person
has the freedom to choose to create good or evil.

Will all humans eventually evolve to be perpetuators of goodness—
citizens in divine world of Peace—
OR
will some people be collected
into that vision of divine peace
while others will remain in a burning darkness of negative energy?
?
?
?

My compassionate heart says
"No one can be content
to live in a divine world of peace
while there are other people
who are suffering in the burning darkness of negativity."

…

Yet, I find that my light of love and peace can get full of ugly black smoke
when I remain too long in the proximity of people perpetuating negative energy.

Sometimes
Life
gives you
rotten lemons—
you can not make
lemonade from those—
you just
have to
throw them away
let them
rot
and hope
that natural law will
make them
into fertilizer
for
something good
to grow later.

I thank the persons in my life who pushed for my failure in order
to feel their success, for they have taught me the lessons of
Justice.

Focus on the meaningful goal.

Peace is closely tied in with a practice of non-judgment and respect.

The people who are litigious—
Who judge things as the "right way" and
who relish in maintaining laws—
Close themselves to many people.
Laws are to serve people, not the other way around.
When maintaining the law supersedes caring for the individual,
humanity is lost.

Laws are guidelines—not the end all and be all.

Why do we have judges?
They bring fairness to situations assisted by laws but not
ruled by them. That is the purpose of a judge.

The purpose of a water pitcher is to hold water.
When it fails to do so, its purpose is lost and it can remain on
the shelf collecting dust or be recycled into something useful.

When we (anyone and everyone) lose connection with our core purpose,
we act as purposeless objects.
We can take on alternative purposes in outer layers like changing clothes.
We can take on a purpose of performing well in a
career, or attaining some material object.

When those purposes are attained,
then what is our purpose?

We change into another set of clothing—
like another occupation
or another material thing to attain.

What happens if you fail in performing well
in a career or attaining an object?
What happens when you lose your job and your finances crash?

What happens when you've lost sight of your core purpose
and only know the outer purposes?
Like a broken pitcher, you throw your life away
as many have done with distractions.

Jealousy is the unwillingness to step forward to become better at loving.

RESPONSIBILITY

Responsibility

How does responsibility relate to Peace?

Responsibility is a companion of freedom. When we take responsibility for our actions, we are free to act. We are free to act when we know that we can accept the consequences. When the consequences are unfavorable, we accept the challenge to take action toward a favorable direction. We do not shy away from difficulty or hard work. We redirect our energies toward our goal; plowing through whatever obstacles there may be.

Letting go of responsibility that is not ours is also freedom. I am not responsible for other's actions and reactions. I am only responsible for mine. While we affect each other, I choose my thoughts, make my mouth talk, and move my body. I may choose to adapt someone else's idea, yet, I choose. While I share my ideas, I expect other's to make their choices that resonate with their truth. I asked in the beginning of this book, "Why do you want to write this book with me?" The thoughts I share come from my life lessons. My intention is to stimulate your wisdom from your life lessons. I am responsible for what I build. You are responsible for your creation. Yet, we can appreciate how we inspire one another. Owning our responsibility gives us the freedom to explore life from a new perspective—freedom to try new things—because we know that whatever mess we get ourselves into, we'll get ourselves out. We also let others get out of their messes, too, although we do not do their work for them.

Look at the situations that you perceive to be your responsibility. Define what you did to create that situation. If you find that you did not create the situation, you may not feel responsible. You can still participate as part of the solution, but beware not to get distracted from your primary responsibility. Sometimes we are unaware of our responsibility in situations. The best approach is to always focus on creating positivity, though we might still make mistakes. Focus on positive goals and solutions will come.

List your perceived responsibilities and how they were created:

Responsibility	How the responsibility was created

Letting go of responsibilities that are not yours means letting go of mental preoccupation. Complaining is often a way of avoiding responsibility. Only when complaint is aimed at getting a result is it part of taking responsibility.

Looking back and turning into a pillar of salt is looking at the past to the point where it takes the life out of you The moisture that gives flexibility is gone. The flow of the ocean is gone. The water is evaporated so only the hardened minerals are left. The life lessons remain hardened and crumble—as stiff as laws in a rulebook. The heart's desire, which is the flow of life, is gone. The innocence of the moment is lost. Living a life by hardened standards is not living. It is standing still as time and life pass by.

Many religions have turned people into pillars of salt through their rigid regulations. The scriptures contain stories of heroes who lived by their hearts. The ancestors of Jesus, especially King David, lived in the flow of a loving God and they could break the commonly accepted interpretations of laws . (i.e. David taking the holy bread from the alter to eat, 1 Samuel 3-6) The women broke sexual rules at the risk of their lives when they carried God's heart. (For example, Tamar in Genesis 38) Mary, who succeeded in birthing Jesus, is a great example of living in the flow of God's heart and risking her life against the hardened rules that humans attributed to God (John 8:5).

I even feel a little crusty after explaining my past experiences, which led me to my current decisions. I tried to explain my situation to a friend who lives by the rules of commonly accepted correctness. Conforming to acceptable rules and guidelines slows my flow. The flow of living in the present is the flow of love. The heart's desire gets slowed as I look for crystallized stones of reasoning that will conform to current human laws and traditions. King David, Mary, and Jesus were definitely not in line with their contemporaries' laws and traditions. They lived in the flow of love, which moves us into a higher realm of consciousness.

As the current moves faster, there is less time to harden my being into reasoning. This is a time of perfecting faith and staying fluid in your heart's energy—a yearning for perfecting true love by being the innocent child with willing openness to flow with the call in your heart. This time will be difficult for people who rely on human reason. They may be left on riverbanks as pillars of salt until a rain comes to wash them into the flow again. They will be further behind those who remained in the flow as we all head toward the ocean of living in the fullness of genuine, original love

I am saddened to leave behind people stuck in human reasoning. I try to engage in reasoning enough to connect them and pull them back into the flow. Each time I do so, I pull out of the flow for the moment. Pulling out of the flow hurts me, but breath gloriously caresses me back into the flow. The grace of breath catches me and carries me when I harden and sink into the mud beneath the flow. My heart calls for the flow. Words in scripture, a person, or an angel lifts me from the mud and back into the flow where I can dissolve and become part of the collective again. My heart calls. Rescuers come. Forgiveness transforms.

Anyone who has hardened and sunken into the dark mud can be rescued with a call from the heart. Then, remain in the flow to be transformed.

"…It is not what goes into the mouth that defiles a person,
but what comes out of the mouth;
this defiles a person" (Matthew 15:11)

HAPPINESS

Perspective

The dog
Chewed up the pillows,
Was put outside,
And is now black with mud.

My child
Is sick with a fever,
Spent days in bed
Missing school.
Doctor thinks the antibiotics
Will help.
I am communicating with teachers.

The workers said
The boards do not fit,
I have to readjust the plan.
The bathroom won't be available
For another three days.

My babysitter is sick.
Groceries are low.
Another grey cloudy day

Life is good.
My broken foot is healing.
Summer is coming.
The family will be together
Tonight.

I'll fix new potatoes and salmon,
Get watercress for the salad,
Fresh berries for desert.

I'll put a small positive
Into this day
How can I manage?
a little prayer
a deep breath
and a call to my friend, Janet

Happiness

Most people pursue happiness as if it were an animal to catch. Chasing happiness is like chasing tomorrow, it's always there, out of reach. Happiness is a state of being. Thoughts move energy in our being, affecting our body and emotions. Some thoughts evoke the experience of happiness. Other thoughts evoke anxiety, depression, laughter, or other states.

Because the state of happiness is a chosen mindset and not an external substance, you have to create it. The following is a meditation that can create happiness:

"Meeting God in Heaven within"

Breathe in to your heart center and lungs—
the breath flows in your whole body
Feel the flow of love saturate you.
Then breathe out the overflow of love
Through your crown chakra (the top of your head) into the universe

You can chant "Q" or "Hu" as in Human. Q or Hu is the sound for God in many near east cultures. Q or Hu is the deified "first word." (Biblically the "Word" is the first step in the process/genesis of all creation) Q or Hu also means "to evoke", "to pour" and "vessel". Q or Hu is one of the three primary sounds in near east cultures and part of many of the names for God (Yahuvahu, Jehovah, Huda, Allahu, Ahura)

You can also chant Sat Nam. Sat Nam means "truth is my identity," You recognize yourself (and others) as truth beings with each breath. "Sat" is voiced in the exhale and "Nam" is either voiced or silently heard on the inhale. This chant acts as a cleanser to remove layers of interpretations and untruths that distort our resonance in our true being.

Sounds are powerful mind cleansers. You can use the sound of your own name as a chant to connect to your true being. Research the roots of your name and connect to a meaning that defines you.

For example, my name "Suna" has the roots "Su" and "Na." "Su" exists in many languages meaning: fire, water, being, belonging, the mother Earth, good, God. "Su"merian is one of the most ancient known languages. "Na" means consort, partner, or spouse. I found the meaning of my name to be "yearning and returning to the love source (God)" also "longing and belonging." Using my name as a chant—"Su" breathing in, as in longing or yearning, and "na" releasing breath out, as in filled in belonging, brings me Peace.

Research your name, meditate and find your truth being in the chant of your name.

Your Name _____

Break down the roots and their meanings:

_____   _____

_____   _____

_____   _____

Your interpretation of your name (Choose your own meaning.):

You breathe all day long. You place love and light in your being all day long. There is no showdown battle, no one major event, and no one time turning point. The renewal is repeatedly fresh and new in the now—this moment. This is a flow of love and light. The flow of love and light spills over from your being to your interactions with the outside world; fear and ignorance are replaced by love and light.

Breathe.

There is a daily life that runs hour to hour in a line from a beginning to an end point; and there is a life of now—existing long before my birth—before my grandmother's mother had a name. It exists in the life of my grandchildren's children as well. The life of now is where we meet regardless of where our feet stand.

It's wonderful when the life of now and daily life connect—like good friends. Daily life is a continuum of changes that writes interesting histories.

Daily life calls you to move.

New Being (New Peace Being)

Falling Apart

I feel that anxiety of trying to make things work.
The more I think, the more hopeless I feel.
I notice that I have two choices:
1. Work harder at making my dreams/goals happen or
2. Fall apart.

In the state of anxiety
when I am trying to make things work, my meditation,
prayers, and spiritual practices do not center me.
Falling apart is what brings me to my center.
Falling apart like an infant needy state, recognizing what I do not know and
that I can not live without others caring for me is like falling into a safety net—
a grounded security.

Perhaps falling apart is deep trust in God—
the primal force of love.

My image
of this emotional falling apart is the crumbling of the Tower of Babel.
I feel like my falling apart is one brick loosened from the Tower wall,
tumbling to the ground.

I am okay with falling apart.

Although my logical mind tells me I am going in the opposite direction of
my goals and dreams, my heart says, "You're okay. Love is carrying you."
I have to reason that if love is carrying me,
I will reach my true heart's desire,
not my picture of it.

I find a delicate balance
between mapping out steps toward goals
and falling apart into the hand of a higher power.

I fell to my hopeless zero this morning—
into a state of trusting peace.
I turn to my trusted friends.
I continue to breathe.
I make momentary choices of action,
trusting the flow of the love force.
That love force pushes me out of bed
to get dressed
and eat breakfast now.
I enjoy letting the love flow lead my life dance.

New Being

The life cycle includes the joy of birth and the grief of death. When I see life as a cycle, I see endings and beginnings meeting in the same point. As an infant departs from his comfortable life in the mother's womb, he is born into a world of faces that love him and that he grows to love. Perhaps as we die after our life in the womb of the earth, we are born into a world of greater potential for love, too. The life cycle also includes the middle parts of life, achieving, growing and living—the cycle between birth and death.

Passover and Easter are available to us every day. There are constant reminders that we can break out of our shells of inhibitions and emerge as new life.

Coming out of Egypt and leaving our prisons of guilt are the moments of new life and new opportunities. What more appropriate visual metaphor can there be than a chick breaking out of its shell?

First, recognizing the territory of inhibitions in which we dwell through awareness gives us the motivation to crack through that shell. The territory of inhibitions may be relationship dynamics, unfulfilled desires that we lack courage to achieve, or a distorted philosophy or interpretation imprisoning our true expression. Only in a quiet, nonjudgmental moment will our unconscious reveal the reality of our pharaohs to us. Once we are aware of the captor of our true being and the fulfillment of joy in life, we can prepare ourselves for the journey.

Recognizing our imprisonment and wanting to escape creates agitation. Agitation creates movement. Movement disturbs the status quo. The status quo resists and pushes against us. When the going gets tough, the tough get going. Getting going takes strength and effort—endurance, too. The chick is not out of the shell until she breaks completely through and steps away from the shell, leaving it forever. Those who followed Moses had a difficult time leaving the shell of Egypt. It took forty years and a new generation to feel at home outside that shell. The process of breaking into new life requires all of one's efforts and focus. All the old norms die away. Jesus spoke about this and finally succeeded in conveying this message when he gave us a visual, tangible experience in his own death on the cross.

The message and the experience of breaking through into new life can happen simply. Gaining awareness of our shells of inhibitors is our actual awakening. Beginning to make the changes is the process. Going consistently forward, out of the old and into the new is the efficient way to reach the new quickly—whether in three weeks or even three days. Wavering back and forth can take forty years or forty generations.

Letting the old die away makes the new possible. Thank heavens that my tulips, lilies, and daffodils died last summer so that the new ones could bloom now in spring.

New life can begin again and again. I look at my children every spring and see a new being in them. The newborn beings were precious, but I was also happy when they could walk. As toddlers, they were so cute and entertaining, and yet, I was glad to get rid of the diapers. The preschool children were absolutely adorable, but I felt such great fulfillment when their minds became very active and I could have real conversations with them. They continue to reinvent themselves into new beings every year. I hope that I, too, am renewing myself into a new being each year, bringing greater joy and love into the world.

Passover, Easter, and spring remind us of new life. May we all break out of our old shells and step into the world as new beings. May we appreciate the new beings in ourselves and in others, as we do in our children. May we all bring greater joy and love into the world starting from within our own beings. Whatever holiday or tradition you celebrate to express this newness, Happy New Being!

The process of "creating self" is both fully in your control and directed by universal principles. Choices of action have consequences that abide by universal principles. Actions that violate universal principles get answered with universal principles. Natural law simply exists, whether we are conscious of it or not. You are a self with potential to develop into greater self. You choose your pace and your expression. What you create within the universal principles will become eternal; all else eventually wears away. You are destined to express your true self.

May we who are blessed
be fair and caring.
May all people be cared for
and blessed through one another.

About the Author
(Back to the Beginning)

As you have answered the questions in the Introduction, I, too, shall introduce myself.

My name is Suna, meaning a yearning and returning to the origin of love. Born in Milwaukee, WI, I was then moved to the Paducah, KY area at age two. Six years later my family moved to Titusville, FL. After a year, we moved again to Charleston, WV, where we remained until both my younger sister and I graduated from high school. I graduated at the age of sixteen, then left my immediate family to live with my uncle's family in Kungalv, Sweden. I spent the next two and a half years in Sweden between Kungalv and Skovde (both near to Gothenberg). I spent summers in the wooded region of northern Sweden. At nineteen I moved to Morgantown, WV to attend West Virginia University for two and a half years, where I received a BA in French with minors in Political Science and German. I spent my senior year of college in Caen, Normandy, France (but spent three or four days of each week in Paris training in modern dance and ballet). After graduating I moved to New York, NY to work at the UN. My fate changed and I pursued dance further until I got into the fashion and acting industries. After getting back to my deep interest in child development through teaching after-school gymnastics and preschool classes, I decide to get a master's level education in the area of psychology and human development. Research into where I could get the best education for my interests led me to New York University's Silver School of Social Work. I received a deep and well-rounded education in individual, family, and group therapy.

I worked in several outpatient clinics on teams with other clinicians educated in social work, psychology, and psychiatry. My clients sought treatment for schizophrenia, multiple personality disorder, depression, marital conflict, substance abuse, developmental delay, AIDS, and other chronic illnesses that brought about mental illness. I realized that a beautiful and genuine human being lives beneath each illness or disorder. Seeing the true person beneath the trauma created a desire in me to work more in early childhood development. Concurrent with my move from New York City to the suburbs into a bedroom community called Chappaqua, NY, I began raising twins and creating a specialized preschool developmental class. I plan to launch my first of a series of children's books based on my developmental class in 2013.

Even though as a baby, my Swedish grandmother took care of me and only spoke Swedish, most of my life I grew up speaking American English. My early language development included both Swedish and the English as a second language that my parents spoke. I count English, Swedish, and French as my fluent languages. I can relate to most Indo-European languages, especially Germanic and romance languages, fairly well. My attempts to learn Russian, Korean, and Turkish took great effort until I decided that I had to approach them as if I were an infant with no prior language. Then unused parts of my brain connected with the new thought structures. I have been studying Jesus's teachings with David Fastiggi, who knows and explains the ancient Aramaic that Jesus spoke. My experience trying to learn a non-Indo-European language helped me understand the mental and emotional shift necessary in order comprehend the deeper meaning in Jesus' words from the Aramaic teachings.

My heart's desire is to reverse the division of people centered on language. I picked up dialects in order to belong with the people around me. Growing up in Kentucky, Florida, and West Virginia, gave me a southern accent. I started to use the "you'ums" of Pittsburgh (near Morgantown) when I moved to that area. In Europe, my English becomes more British. For the most part I try to enunciate in a way that I will be understood.

My family background is diverse. My father was born and raised in Turkey. His mother was born to a government representative during the Ottoman Empire living in Bulgaria. The family moved to Istanbul at the fall of the empire around World War I. My father's father was a plantation owner in central Turkey, who was born to a mother from Caucasus Mountains in current day Georgia (formally part of the Soviet Union). I believe my blond and fair great-grandmother on my father's Turkish side is the reason why I look Scandinavian like my mother's side of the family. My mother is pure Swedish.

I am the older of two daughters and often felt to be my father's son. I helped him build shelves. He took me shooting, hiking, and exploring. Yet, he had a Middle Eastern attitude toward women, so I was expected to be good at serving, cooking, and taking care of children. Being the oldest, I was the one who trained my parents to be parents in every stage of their development and mine. My father often asked me for advice in guiding my sister who is three years younger. (She was allowed to do much more than I was.) As the eldest, I gained a close, experiential understanding of my parent's culture.

Traditions I have:

I celebrate Thanksgiving in America. The New Year on January first is a day of new intention for me. The Christian holidays, such as Christmas and Easter, have always been celebrated in my family. I connect with the Jewish holidays of Rosh Hashanah, Yom Kippur, and Passover as well as the Muslim month of fasting, Ramadan. Traditionally, I go to the gym four mornings of the week and e-mail or call my closest friends daily: I tell my children I love them daily and my mother frequently. My regular routines change in response to other life changes.

My closest relationships:

My closest relationships are within my generation. I find a respectful boundary of experience between generations. I love my parent's generation with a reverence for their struggle to create the foundation on which I stand. I collected many friends from around the world whom I can trust and depend on. Some friends are always spiritually, mentally, and emotionally available. Others are, additionally, physically available.

My favorite things to do:

I love doing projects with other people—being productive physically, mentally, spiritually, and emotionally. I love dance, music, painting, and writing! I seem to have an overabundance of thoughts that need to get out in order not to feel frustrated. I love deeply communing, whether in a prayer walk through the woods, creating artwork, a social lunch, or sharing intimate moments.

How I spend my day:

I lay in bed for a while after I wake, read messages of inspiration and e-mails from my closest friends, and write (both in my journal and to my closest friends). When I get up, I throw on gym clothes and drive to a beautiful clean gym in Armonk, ten minutes away. I use a machine that makes me breathe heavy and sweat while talking with a friend there or watching Kelly Ripa, who makes me laugh. The exercise, sweating, and laughing are the best psychiatric medicine that I have discovered to counteract the stress of life. After the gym, I keep going from one task to the other. Daily activity takes up a lot of time—cleaning, cooking, eating, and taking care of the little responsibilities. Some days I teach, while other days I work on projects, such as this book, educational groups, or my friend's documentary film. I socialize.

The five most important things to me are

1) Connecting with the source of life and love (by whatever name you call it);
2) Developing healthy relationships;
3) Developing myself into a trustworthy, true, loving person—developing my true being more and more;
4) Inspiring others to become fully who they truly are; and
5) Giving children the best opportunity to develop into healthy beings.

Introductions provide just a little information. Relationship interactions reveal who we truly are. We describe ourselves as we wish to see ourselves. Others describe how we have affected them. Somewhere in-between how we describe ourselves and how others describe us is a fluid reality of our identities.

We are both accomplishments and potential, driven by our desires. We discover our priorities by observing where we devote our energy. Sometimes we have opposing hopes. For example, a person may say, "I want to stop smoking." Then ten minutes later, he or she lights a cigarette and smokes it. The person expresses one wish and follows another. If the person fully wants to stop smoking, he or she would invest his energy into something he or she wants to start. Then there is no energy being put into the smoking habit. (Habits have momentum and require a strong, mindful energy to move away from them.)

I yearned to write this book with you and now we have completed our story. We have a "scripture" of reminders that will help bring clarity in moments of confusion. Just like Mother Nature created every herb and plant that can bring health to our physical bodies, universal truths expose themselves in our life experiences to help us grow a healthy spirit. This text is designed to be a stimulus, prompting us to collect and record the truths revealed throughout our days. As I become disturbed and confused from certain situations, I need rebalancing, which I get from Holy Scriptures, words of wisdom, and my journals. We recorded some of our most meaningful insights in this keepsake.

Thank you

Thank you to the following people:

Jennifer Crumpley, who combed through two versions of my manuscript to give me corrections so that you could read this book more easily.

David Fastiggi, who helped me develop ideas and kept me sane by talking with me daily.

Stephanie Walker, who carved out time in her busy life to proofread this book and give her youthful, intelligent perspective.

Maureen Jacobson of Monad Marketing, for her insights on expression.

Beryl Hay, Bernadette Bloom, Shahnaz Fahra, Barbara Vahsen, Marina Lebedinets, Elizabeth Kemler, Susan Shopkorn, Lance McGinnis, John Zagar, Johanna StMichaels, Charlotte Hoije, Janet Stephens, Elder Fuller, Jane Margolin, and Kathie Hall, who gave me extra support when I needed it.

My many wonderful friends who are my lab partners in life—learning to be trustworthy, respectable, forgiving, and good friends together with me.

You—for creating this book together with me and taking steps together toward building a world of peace. Let's revisit our wisdom regularly and keep walking into *Peace: Discovering Life's Harmony through Relationships*.